I Teach Middle School

A Survivor's Tale: How to Understand Middle School Students so you can Reach them.

Heather Burrbridge

ISBN: 9798666281376

Photo Design: Jean Paul Pando
Additional Art Support: Deanna Lethbridge and Green Leaf Graphics.

Printed in the United States of America.

Free Resource

Thank you for purchasing my book. I want to help you become the amazing teacher you are meant to be. The first step is to set your classroom up for success and then later learn to communicate effectively with parents.

Use the following link to get a copy of your FREE classroom checklist and email shells for those difficult parent emails.

https://landing.mailerlite.com/webforms/landing/d5m5s5

Dedication

To my first and most influential teacher, my mom. You found a way to teach thousands of students and your own children with levels of grace and compassion that I will always admire.

Table of Contents

Preface

I have always felt called to be an educator, but when I entered the classroom it was not what I expected. The demands, behaviors, and constraints of education are driving teachers out of the classroom. I want to inspire other teachers to rise above the challenges in order to make the difference we were meant to make in the world. With small adjustments in expectations and management you can be the great teacher that middle school students need.

Introduction: All About Me

I am a left-handed, mom of two, Type B, Disney freak, disorganized teacher. I laugh when I tell people I teach middle school because I love the mixture of pure horror on someone's face of *"Why would I want to do that?"*, and the look of admiration when people think, *"How do you do it?"* The reactions of others and the number of interactions I deal with in a single day made me realize that being a successful middle school educator requires the skills of a trained ninja. Like a ninja you must be constantly alert, planning your next move, and being ready for anything that comes your way.

My teaching/ninja training journey is a bit unique. I can't imagine teaching anything but middle school, and I have spent the majority of my career serving as a teacher in the very same middle school I attended as an obnoxious pre-teen. I was inspired to go into teaching because of two amazing teachers in my life. The first and most influential role model was my mom, a retired teacher who still likes working with kids after 30+ years in education and still subs in the local schools. God bless her! The only person braver than a middle school teacher is someone willing to be a substitute. My second influence was my 4th grade teacher, who helped me through a difficult time at school when I was behind with my reading skills and didn't have any friends in my class. She got me hooked on science and I eventually became a middle school Science teacher. I still think of her when I plan mystery labs for my class the way she used to do for me.

True Fact: I never pictured myself teaching middle school as I am an elementary education major. I stayed up at night picturing the perfect themed elementary classroom where I would make lasting memories with a small group of students. My mom encouraged me to choose a minor in another subject (I chose Science) and then took the Praxis in Middle School Science to have more opportunities when it came to getting a job. When I graduated and applied to teach in my home district in the county I grew up in, I started getting calls just days after graduation. I didn't realize at first that all of the schools calling me were middle schools. I was just so excited to have schools who wanted to interview me. I accepted a position teaching 6th grade science at a school in my childhood school district. (I found out later that HR had only placed my resume in middle school because of the high need area. Coincidence? I think not.)

I was feeling extra confident walking into my first year of teaching based on success in my college classes and the large number of schools who had reached out to me for interviews. I wanted to make a difference for students and help them stay engaged in learning. Within a few short months, my confidence faded and I was crying on the couch from stress with the worst case of bronchitis I have ever had that forced me to be out of school for a whole week. My mom helped me adjust my expectations about the overwhelming realities of being in the classroom. I had to take a step back and get perspective on the things I could and could not control. Long story short, I stayed in teaching. During these years I have figured out some survival tips that I hope to share with you. If you are looking for modern research and statistics, this is not the place for you. I pride myself on being honest and sharing my perspective: what I have seen with my own eyes in my 15+ years in the classroom. I hope you can relate to some of my ideas and rest assured that you are not the only one struggling with the demands and behaviors of teaching in middle school.

Me as a Middle School Student

Congratulations, you have survived your awkward middle school years and become a functional adult! If you now have the bravery to go back and deal with middle school from the other side of the desk, you may want to take a journey back to your own experience to understand the students you see in your room.

At first glance you might not really have memories from middle school. That could be for several reasons, maybe you hated everything and nothing stuck, or maybe you blocked it out of your long-term memory. If you look closely, I believe middle school plays a big part as you realize who you are going to become.

If I had to describe my middle school self in a few words they would be….

Competitive: Competing was a big part of my life in middle school. First, I was passionate about playing softball and I wanted to be the best player on the best team. I played catcher and first base, and I loved winning. My team would wear our jerseys to school on game days. There was another team in my league full of the "popular" girls. I think my whole team brought their A game on those days as a chance to really feel good about beating them every time we played them. I would become so angry when we would lose, and my Dad and I would rehash all of the plays of the game that could have changed the outcome.

Creative: In 7th grade, my middle school started offering high school credit to students if you wanted to take a foreign language in middle school. I had no interest in language and wasn't interested in pushing myself to get ahead in high school. Instead I took a creative writing class. One assignment was to watch the movie *Ferris Bueller's Day Off* and then write my own narrative on what I would do if I had a skip day from school. The assignment was so fun and allowed me to engage a different part of my brain.

Leader: During my time in middle school I started a trend that would continue well into high school. I would take the small network of friends that I brought from elementary school and slowly bring in stray students who didn't have a group of friends. It was a good approach to making friends because it put me in the constant position as leader. I liked to be the one who made the decisions like whether someone should sit with us at lunch, or what country we should research for a group project. When it came to my best friend who lived in my neighborhood, I would be caught saying phrases like, "If you don't want to do what I want to do then just go home".

Leadership can sometimes be confused with power. I would test my teachers by sitting where I wanted or talk when we were supposed to be doing independent work. When they would redirect me, sometimes I wanted to show that I wasn't afraid of them so I would be sassy or difficult just to show that I was a leader. Other students laughing would of course encourage me to puff up my chest a bit fuller. I wasn't a bad student; I got all A's and B's, but sometimes I just wanted to show what I was capable of.

Unsure: The outside appearance certainly showed leadership and confidence. That was probably a facade for how I was feeling on the inside. I remember that in the 6th grade, the county school system offered an overnight field trip (Outdoor Education) where all of the learning took place outdoors. This was a once in a lifetime chance that I almost missed because I was terrified to spend the night at someone's house much less at some weird camping facility. My mom saved the day as a chaperone so I wouldn't miss out. Of course, I probably told my friends I don't know why my mom wanted to chaperone; I would have never admitted the truth on that one.

I have several other memories that may not point to specific character traits but they seem to fit with a typical middle school experience. I remember that my best friend and I would be dropped off at the end of our half mile driveway to catch the bus in the morning. I remember when there was a substitute bus driver, one or two students on the bus would tell the bus driver we didn't ride that bus and the driver would drive past us. That made me so angry because of course those kids were just jerks, and pissed because I was not being accepted and I had to walk the half mile back to my house to figure out a way to get to school.

I remember middle school being the start of boyfriends and girlfriend drama. This was the start of phrases like, *"Do you like him or do you like like him?"* I had a boyfriend who never ate lunch with me or sat next to me in class. We did go on a date to see the original *Toy Story*. (Yes, I am well aware that I am dating myself with this detail.) During our "date", my mom and sister sat somewhere else while me and my date sat with another couple in our own seats. We were so in love and of course so mature.

One of the last memories I have is the day I was vacuuming the bathroom and I accidentally vacuumed up a pair of my red underwear. This was one of the only bold colored pairs I had gotten in my pack of brand name underwear. I spent quite a bit of time trying to take apart the vacuum and rescue the underwear so I wouldn't have to tell my dad about the incident. Even thinking about confronting him was absolutely humiliating.

All of these memories are so random so why would I bother sharing them with you? First, who we are in middle school marks the beginning of our character that takes shape and we grow into as an adult. I would still use some of these same words to describe myself today, but hopefully I am using those attributes for good and not for my own gain.

Competitive: I have started to change my competition with competing against myself more than I compete with others. Some of my joy used to be beating others so I could win. Now I usually want everyone to win, like when I get belts in Tae Kwon Do, I'm proud of others that also get their belts for their hard work. Occasionally I slip into my old competitive habits and pout a little when my husband wins at board game night for the 4th week in a row, but I mostly control my competitive edge.

Creative: I love to write, journal, scrapbook, take pictures and paint. Projects that are hands on give me a great outlet for some of my excess emotional energy and I love to use this creativity to help myself. I share my creativity with others.

Leader: I have served in many leadership roles in my time as a teacher. I really like to encourage others to work together and do what's best for students. I am not afraid to stand up for what is right. I have also found leadership positions outside of work in some of the volunteer activities I participate in. Recently, I have realized my own limitations that even though I am a leader, I need to say no to some commitments that stretch me too thin. My personality says I want to be in charge, but my logical brain says you can't lead everything.

Unsure: My challenges of fitting in and making friends still continues as an adult. I have had more than a few cries to my mom and husband about the fact that I don't have any friends, or I wish I could get in better shape. Now I have two kids, and there's always a level or uncertainty when it comes to parenting. As soon as I feel like I master a phase like preschool, the kids move on to elementary school. My insecurities rise to surface at work, and at home because I 'm human.

Think About It: I challenge you to take a trip down memory lane. What words would you use to describe your middle school self? How are those words similar or different to you as an adult?

I wasn't an unruly kid in middle school, I was just an annoying early teenager like the rest of you. It's important to remember that growing out of some of our less than endearing behaviors was partially thanks to the adults in our lives who modeled appropriate behaviors, set boundaries for us, accepted us and invested in us. We have the chance to do the same for the students we teach today. Knowing that middle school students have brains and behaviors that are under construction, we can be the steady adult who gives support with boundaries. We can accept their flaws knowing that just like us, they will make it through these awkward years and turn into a functional adult.

Why would I bother to include these irrelevant old memories from years ago? In each of these glimpses from the past we see a bit of what it means to be a middle schooler. I remember times when I felt good about myself, new experiences and experiences that were totally embarrassing. I have very few memories in between. Most middle schoolers remember these same types of experiences.

Another reason I think these memories are important is because as adults we have such a different lens for viewing situations than middle school students do. If we can remember how they view the world and what's important to them, we can do better teaching them in the classroom.

Here are some things that were true for me as a 13-year-old, and are still true for most middle schoolers I know:

- Kids in middle school want to act independent and grown up, but they still need their parents
- Some kids are jerks (and we were probably jerks too!)
- Middle school is the time of many first loves, hormones, body changes and being awkward
- Students are focused on what is important to them: friends, sports, extracurricular activities, (learning and school are not always the most important in their brain)
- Students embarrass easily and everything is a big deal to them
- Students want to fit in and find friends who will accept them
- Middle school students test boundaries but they really need structure and boundaries to feel safe

Chapter 1: Welcome to Middle School!

It may have been a while since you stepped foot in a middle school. You may be asking, what does a typical day in middle school look like? Well for starters, when you are dealing with 600-900 preteens there is no typical day. If you are someone who gets bored easily, working in a middle school may be perfect for you. Sit back and try to visualize middle school. First, the staff starts to come to life around 7:30 as computers are turned on, and coffee is brewing. Teachers take a few deep breaths enjoying a few minutes to collect their thoughts.

The bell rings, meaning the school doors are opening. Students bike, and walk to school, but the majority of them arrive by bus. Fifty students at a time filter through the front doors with noise levels that make you wonder how many students are in the halls. You have some students looking like zombies who barely woke up enough to get on to the school bus, and others who look like they have been up for an hour working on their hair and outfit. Students are supposed to go to their locker and then right to class, but they just group together with similar friends. You see small collections of students gathering at one locker that has a width of 12 inches. As four to five students share the space, other students are blocked from accessing their own locker. Most locker interactions are peaceful and students wait till the groups disperse. Teachers who are on locker duty get caught up with the smell of too much strange cologne, breakfast pastries and a small bit of middle school body odor. Ah the smells of middle school.

There is always some excitement from events that were shared over social media that need to be worked out in the morning and shared with anyone who missed out on the latest updates. Teachers are always in the dark about all of these happenings and start the day being cell phone police. We remind students that we are back in school and we need to put down hoods, phones away, and turn their voices back to indoor voices. This is how we start every single day for the entire school year. At times teachers contemplate making a recording of themselves saying these key phrases so they won't have to strain their voice with the same repetitive talk. Just when teachers are about to burst, the bell rings for students to get to class.

Students start moving quickly in all directions. Lockers are closed and the crowd of students thins down to lower concentration. Once the students enter the classroom, it takes a minute or two for their brains and bodies to settle and then the environment is totally different.

Lesson learned: Don't judge a middle school by the chaos during transition times. Life in the halls and the classroom are totally different. I remember my husband coming to drop off something to me at dismissal one time and asking me if I was safe at my school. From an outsider's perspective it makes sense to feel a little stressed over transitions. Insiders know transitions are times when kids are burning off some excess energy from all their learning, and acting like kids with freedom.

Basic Middle School Structures

Now that you get a mental picture of the beginning of the day, you can now see what the rest of the day looks like in a middle school setting. If you walk into a public middle school you will typically see students in grades 6-8 which means that the students usually range in ages from 11-14 years of age. Middle school students typically have seven classes per day that they rotate through during each day. Each class is typically taught by a different teacher in a different classroom covering a different subject. Teachers are divided into departments that they teach including: Math, Science, Social Studies, Foreign Language, English and Language Arts, PE, Art and Electives, and Technology. Teachers typically stay within their own classrooms and different groups of students come and go within their space for about 45-60 minutes. Students do not have a home based classroom where they keep their belongings, instead most middle schools have lockers for students where they will stop at first thing in the morning to drop off backpacks and coats, and then they will go back to their lockers throughout the day to get materials they need and then at the end of the day to retrieve their bigger items. As students move through the school with bells that indicate their time to move, they carry a basic 3 ring binder and school supplies.

As a teacher, you typically teach four to five different groups of students during the day. Depending on the size of your school, most teachers plan for one to three preps, which means different classes. For example, you may teach two different grade level classes like 6th grade science and 7th grade science. Classes range between twenty-five and thirty students. In middle school, students in a grade level take the same core classes and then they have a choice of their elective and possibly one other class during the day. Some classes in middle school such as Math and Foreign Language are leveled and students enter classes that are appropriate to their learning and readiness levels, where other subjects are taught at the same level to everyone at a grade level. At my school all students in a grade level take the same science and social studies classes.

Middle school teachers in my district arrive in middle school through one of two avenues. Some teachers are secondary education majors that focused on one specific subject and they are an expert in their content. Other teachers are elementary education majors that found a certain subject they really enjoyed and decided to teach middle school. Both of these backgrounds can work for middle school if you understand the unique middle school environment. If you are considering a job in middle school, you typically focus on a content area that you are interested in teaching. As I mentioned, certain departments may be more likely to teach multiple levels, so that can be a consideration when choosing a subject that you are interested in. For example, the music teacher in middle school is going to be responsible for teaching all different levels of band as well as orchestra. They may have three preps. Other content teachers like science and social studies are more likely to have fewer preps because more students take the same core class.

One of the challenges with being either a secondary or elementary education major and teaching middle school is that you need to understand the differences of students in the early adolescence of middle school compared to elementary or high school students. Middle school students have their own unique needs. They are more independent readers and can show more academic stamina. They still need a lot of structure and content specific skills need to be taught. They need guidance to start tasks because they are still learning executive functioning. They also need check points for extended projects. High schoolers are more independent learners compared to middle school learners. If you are interested in middle school, you need to understand the development of their specific age group.

Teaching Middle School versus Elementary School

I am a teacher with a major in elementary education with a minor in middle school education. I did my student teaching in both elementary and secondary schools. Thanks to my mom's insightful advice, I am certified to teach at both the elementary and middle school levels. In my 15-year teaching career, I have taught as an elementary classroom teacher, an elementary specialist, a middle school classroom teacher and a middle school team leader (a fancy title for a full-time teacher who teaches one less class and serves as a backup administrator, meeting planner, and dean of students)

Based upon my years of experience, I can point out the basics of each position, along with the pros and cons of each position so that you can see which level is best for you.

Elementary Classroom Teacher:
In a typical elementary classroom, you teach in a central homeroom with a group of 20-30 students. They spend the majority of the day with you covering all of the core subjects, English Language Arts, Math, Science, Social Studies and Spelling. Students in my county rotate throughout the grade level for differentiated math. Every school and district structure the classrooms differently, but that is the general idea. You have control over how you set up the classroom with decorations, management systems, and discipline procedures. You are given choices on how to assess homework, grading and how you will teach a variety of subjects. Since you have the students all day it is easy to assign classroom jobs where students can help maintain and take pride in their classroom. Typically, an elementary classroom teacher will have planning at the same time with other grade level teachers so they can work on planning for instruction as a team.

Elementary education majors spend a lot of time learning how to teach and differentiate lessons, how to instruct a reading group, and how to use age appropriate child psychology techniques so that they are prepared to face many of these obstacles in the classroom. Elementary teachers are experts on how to teach so they do not always have to be an expert in one particular content. For example, the level to which a student needs to know elementary science and social studies is not a deep level of understanding of each content area.

Elementary school is never boring because you are constantly teaching different objectives for new subjects. However, in order to teach that variety of subjects you have to plan for each subject each day. In my district you plan math, science, writing, reading and spelling every day. Teachers are expected to differentiate their reading groups to meet different students' needs which means balancing four different reading groups in addition to everything else you do.

Elementary school educators get the chance to build a really special relationship with students because you are essentially with these students five hours a day. I still remember each of my elementary teachers so it definitely opens up lasting memories and relationships.

Pros:
- Relationship building opportunities
- Control over discipline, classroom procedures and student expectations
- Teaching a variety of content throughout the day
- Team Planning to help with planning all of the different subjects
- Lunch and Recess for a combined hour teaching break plus specials as additional planning
- Later starting time if you aren't a morning person, or if you like time to work out, sleep in or do errands in the morning

Cons:
- Many subjects to plan for daily

- Five hours a day with students who may challenge your nerves
- Constant revisiting of teaching to help students make progress
- Later dismissal affecting doctor's appointments and afternoon commutes
- Paperwork, data collection and meetings for students with accommodations for students going through evaluative testing
- Lots of different transitions, changing of subjects and organization required

Middle School Teacher:
    As I mentioned already, middle school teachers are typically teaching one or two subjects with different groups of students. Each class meets for approximately forty-five minutes and then when the bell rings the students move to another teacher and a new subject. As a middle school teacher, you are the expert of your subject area and usually have 1-2 other teachers who teach the same subject area who will plan with you with during the week. Since I only have to prepare for two different classes, I can plan really great lessons that run smoothly. Throughout the day since I repeat the lesson over, I can make changes to improve my lesson throughout the day. Usually, I have only one handout a day per class, making it easier to have organization in my classroom. My school has a 7-period day so I teach 5 periods and have one period of meetings/collaborative planning/conferences and one 45-minute period a day for individual planning time.

    The elephant in the room about middle school is the behaviors and attitudes of the students. Middle schoolers sometimes live up to the stereotype of behaviors, but most students can be redirected to learning if learning is engaging and the classroom is managed well. Students need some support with transition time to settle from the hallway excitement and they often need support keeping themselves organized for seven different classes. There are a lot of independent skills that need to be taught. When middle school behaviors do get irritating students only stay in class for 45 minutes and then they leave. I get the chance to see different students throughout the day instead of interacting with the same students over and over again. There are always going to be challenging students, but in middle school, you also have the advantage of other teachers who work with the same student who may be able to share insights and strategies that they have found work in their space. Middle school teams can be a great support system for dealing with the everyday challenges. You do not have as much control over student behavior in other classrooms as there may be different expectations, so you have resistance to following rules if you are the stricter teacher. However, with time and building relationships you can get your classroom running the way you want.

Pros:
- Dismissal occurs early enough if the afternoon to have appointments and other afternoon activities
- Only one content for which to plan
- 45 minutes of individual planning time
- Breaks from students who can be challenging
- Other teachers teach the same students so you can support each other on useful strategies and interventions for students
- Easier to organize and master classroom instruction
- Less paperwork and transitions

Cons:
- Parents are not as involved (can be a pro or a con)
- Lengthier assignments to grade
- Less control over student behavior
- School days begin earlier
- Difficulty with remembering where you stopped for different classes
- Teaching the same lessons four or five times a day can get a little repetitive

Teaching Middle School versus High School

I will be up front in saying that I have never taught high school, so I am writing this based on what I know about the experience from friends and peers that have taught high school. To become a high school teacher, you typically start as a secondary education major in college with a focus on a specific subject as your area of expertise. Other high school teachers may have a degree in a certain subject and then later decide to get a Masters in education. Either of these routes can lead you to a job in a public middle or high school. So, what is the basic difference between middle school and high school? Here are the highlights as I understand.

High school typically covers grades 9-12 with students ranging from 14-18 years old. High schools are divided into departments just like middle schools and typically schools are built with different departments in different areas of the building. Teachers usually teach five sections of students and students move from class to class similar to a middle school setting. A big part of high school is participating in extracurricular activities, so there are countless opportunities to coach or work with clubs and invest in students in ways besides teaching.

High school students have a set number of classes that they have to take in each subject area in order to meet their graduation requirements. For example, they may need four math credits. Unlike middle school, there are more offerings for classes in each subject area. In math alone, a high school might offer Algebra, Algebra II, Geometry, Pre-Calculus, Calculus, Statistics, Finance, Consumer Math and then within each of these classes they may have on-level, honors and AP section of classes. So, within the math department of a middle school there might be six math options, but high school may offer up to fifteen different choices for math classes. As a teacher, this means that in order to meet the students needs you may be teaching a wider variety of classes. In an average middle school, you have more than one teacher teaching the same course. I teach 7th grade science with another 7th grade science teacher. We are expected to plan together and to have our gradebooks aligned so that all 7th graders are getting the same experience and exposure to curriculum. In high schools, most of the time planning with a cohort is not required. This means that if you have a free period you get to work on your own stuff, but it also means you miss out on the ideas of what someone else might do to cut down your planning workload or to get new ideas.

In middle school, you move through the curriculum at a slower pace than high school, and high school instruction is going to delve deeper into a subject. Middle school teachers don't have to have such a deep understanding of their content, and if you are teaching something new you can easily stay ahead of your class. In high schools you really need to understand your content and how to teach it to students. Since I teach science, here is what I mean. My students learn about the food chains and what types of organisms they have in a food chain. We spend two weeks learning about food chains using books, online games and labs and then they take one to two assessments on it. If I was unfamiliar with this topic then I could learn enough to cover the basics for a two-week study in around an hour. The students have very little background knowledge on the topic so I am starting at the ground level. If I teach high school biology, I am covering food chains in one lesson and then I am moving on to the specific nutrients used by decomposers and looking at the energy transfer of organisms in an ecosystem. I am then moving on to graphs to look at the limiting factors that prevent food chains from maintaining their natural balance for the next day. For someone like me who does not have a thorough background in environmental science, I would need to be prepping and really reviewing what I was teaching each day because there is a lot of content to teach.

High school students typically want to graduate, and they cannot graduate without passing all of their classes. This is a big difference between the typical middle school model. In the district where I work, students in middle school typically move on to the next grade even if they have not passed all of their subjects. Since high schoolers want to graduate, you hope that they are more engaged in their learning. This could be a benefit when it comes to classroom management. You also hope that students in high school are more mature than middle school students and they can stay focused longer and work independently.

High School Pros:
- Higher student accountability-they have to pass in order to graduate
- More time to yourself-middle school teachers usually have one period a day for independent planning time and then one meeting a day to focus on collaboration or student behaviors
- Early dismissal time-schools end before 3:00 so you have time to make afternoon

High School Cons:
- More planning if you teach a larger number of different classes
- More grading: higher level classes=equals longer assignments
- Lengthier assignments mean more time grading
- Less collaboration with colleagues
- Early start time-most high schools start around 7:00 am so it might not be a good fit if you are not a morning person

Now you have an idea about elementary, middle and high school. They are all unique learning environments. When you are thinking about what is a good fit for you, think about your lifestyle and interests to see where you fit.

Think About it:
*Are you willing to become a morning person or do you prefer a later start?
*Are you interested in teaching one subject, many subjects, or lots of different topics within one subject?
*Do you want to work on a collaborative team or work more independently?

Different Types of Middle Schools

Every school is different, but there is a definite difference between private and public middle schools. Private middle schools are often joined to an elementary school where the school serves grades K-8. One central administration presides over all of the grade levels. Schools with this model tend to be smaller in size and the structure is more like a typical elementary school where the same group of students would travel together to different subject teachers. Many times, this model is like a tight knit family model, and the students know each other very well but also know how to push each other's buttons. As a teacher in this type of private school model, you will be teaching many different grade levels or subjects because there usually are not enough students to support as many teachers. Private schools are often affiliated with a religious organization like a church and in this model, religion is often part of the school curriculum. Teachers have more freedom in what they teach, but often fewer resources as well. For example, the county I work in has a set curriculum that we can follow and also budgets for science materials. Not every private school has that level of funding. Some teaching positions are considered part time, or without benefits. Many teachers who are not as dependent on the salary like the idea of a private school because it is smaller and they typically have strict rules for student behaviors where students can be removed from school if they do not meet these academic and behavior guidelines.

The other types of middle schools are the public schools where there is a much larger number of students and you have different departments and teams. The salary for public middle school teachers is drastically different across the country, but usually public-school teachers receive benefits if they are full time because we are considered government employees. If you teach in a public school you know that all students are guaranteed the right to a public education, so you can end up with quite a mixed bag of behaviors, personalities and school backgrounds. In a public school just as the students are diverse, the level of parent involvement is also diverse. I have friends of mine who work in a certain school where every time they post a grade online, they get an email from a parent about a grade. I have also seen the other extreme where a large majority of students do not have a parent email on file and the phone mailboxes are full.

> **Think About It:** When it comes to choosing a middle school that is the fit for you, you have to ask yourself some of these questions:
>
> - How much do I want to communicate and work with parents?
> - What kind of behaviors and learning needs can I work with successfully?
> - How many different subjects and preps can I handle teaching?
> - Do I want more freedom in what I teach, or would I prefer a really guided curriculum?

While there is no perfect school when it comes to meeting your needs as a teacher, each school has their strengths and weaknesses. Some schools have higher demands for meetings, collaboration, parent involvement and numbers of teaching preps. All of these should be considerations when making a choice for a school. I have chosen to work in a public setting, because I like the diversity of students and benefits that come with my position. Since my own children are in public school also, my job keeps my family on the same schedule. It works for me, but you have to figure out what works best for you and your family. While there is no perfect school finding a match that works for you will increase your day to day job satisfaction.

Chapter 2: What about the actual middle school student?

Middle School Brain Development

Middle school students grow physically faster than their brain is developing. Their brain looks more like that of an elementary student, where sometimes their body deceives teachers to see someone who looks more like a high school student. In order to be successful in middle school you have to know and understand basics of brain development.

Here are a few comments actually made to me by some of my middle school students; learning about brain development can help you understand the comments and my response.

"Did you get a haircut, it looked better before."
"I hate this whole F*&^\$**g class and I'm leaving."
After being told to have a seat, "You're so racist."

I'm kind of a brain nerd, but here are the basics of what happens to your brain over time. Your brain is living tissue that grows with you as you grow just like your muscles, bones and organs. The difference between your brain and other body parts is that it doesn't just grow, it develops. Growth is getting bigger while development is maturing and changing. There are stages of development where your brain goes through growth spurts just like your physical body. The first major growth spurt is the toddler years. Small children learn to walk, move, talk and other things by using the back parts of their brain that focus on motor skills. Elementary students start using the language part of their brain as they learn to read and write. The elementary students are able to use different parts of their brain at the same time. They use the parts for language, motor skills, and also constantly engage their brain when using their memory. Somewhere between age 6-8, a person's brain has reached its physical size that it will remain for the rest of their life. From that point on, we develop the connections in our brain. Our brain is made of cells, like every other part of your body. The cells in your brain are called neurons. As we learn new skills, we strengthen the neurons. Neurons actually become thicker and more active each time we use them. When students read, they are causing those language neurons to get stronger. They ride a bike and strengthen motor neurons.

When students reach puberty, their brain is going through another growth spurt. Three areas where the brain is developing are abstract thinking, hormones and emotional reasoning.

Abstract Thinking: Students start to make abstract connections instead of only being able to focus on the concrete. The frontal lobe is starting to develop which is where students can think of abstract ideas. Academically, this new development allows them to start to access complex math equations and analyze text. Students in middle school can understand how to solve things like $2x + 4 = 14$ or use equations for solving for density by knowing that Density $=$ Mass x Volume. These equations would be difficult for a developing elementary school brain.

Hormones: Say this in in front of a class of teenagers and you will get a lot of giggling. We think the word is only used to describe changes in teenagers. However, most people misunderstand hormones. Hormones are the chemicals in your body that do work to keep your body healthy. Some hormones tell us when we are sleepy, hungry or when we are scared. Every human at every age has hormones working in their body. So, what is happening with teenage hormones? The most obvious hormonal change occurs when puberty begins and the reproductive hormones from the ovaries and testes kick in. Bodies are changing, growing hair, and the feelings towards sexual thoughts and feelings are in the forefront of the brain. If you have ever taught middle school, you know that students are quick to make sexual connections to words that may not have any sexual innuendo.

As a science teacher here are some vocab words that always cause some laughter and squirming: organism, organelle, ball, equipment, and don't forget any words that involve but, come or hard. Just think through your word choices when you teach middle school.

Hormones are not just about sexuality. Hormones also cause overproduction of oils in the skin that often leads to acne. Other hormones and chemicals in the body shift when a child enters puberty. Melatonin the sleep chemical usually sets in from about 8-9 p.m. for elementary students and around 10 p.m. for adults. With all of their body changes, middle school students don't always feel the effects of melatonin until after midnight. Students don't feel tired as early as they used to in elementary school. This can lead to staying up late and then difficulty getting up in the morning. These hormone changes lead students to be overtired during the week from lack of proper amounts of sleep and then they sleep 12 hours a night on the weekends to catch up. Of course, students make choices like lots of screen time and unhealthy food choices that a lead to sleep problems, but to be fair there are also chemical components to teenage sleep problems.

Emotional Reasoning: Besides changes in hormone levels, students are working on developing a brand-new part of their brain. They are building new neurons that connect their current brain parts to the new frontal lobe of their brain. This part of the brain deals with abstract thought which we already addressed. However, the most important job of the frontal lobe is to make connections from actions to consequences, to control impulses, to process information and to understand the emotions of others. Remember this part of the brain is new construction. There is still metaphorical dust, and construction going on. It works sometimes, but doesn't work other times. It's like the internet that I had back in the late 90's with the old AOL dial up. I remember waiting for over 5 minutes for that connection to fire up. Keep in mind: teenage brain =dial up internet, while the adult brain = high-speed technology.

What does this frontal lobe construction mean for students in middle school? It means that they are impulsive, they make decisions without thinking about what they are doing. They tell you they hate you without thinking of how you will be impacted. They don't even know why they said some unkind words when you go to talk to them about the comment later on in class. Teenagers are very connected to using their amygdala which is their emotional control center. If you say some constructive feedback to them, they are over sensitized with their own feelings, but they can't see your emotions. Talking back, acting out for attention, and other annoying behaviors they show are all part of this new construction. When they escalate a situation in class because they feel threatened, their amygdala is being hijacked by the strong emotion and none of the reasoning of consequences is coming through to their neural connections.

The bad news for middle school students is that the frontal lobe does not complete its construction until students enter their early 20s. The bad news for teachers is that middle school brains are under construction and not everything they do is under their conscious control. Do we let it go? No way. We just need to tread lightly when dealing with students because they are really sensitive to attention, especially in front of their peers. Choose our words carefully, and give them time to calm down and control that oversensitive amygdala before we revert back to our immature primal selves and engage with our emotions. Remember you are an adult, and your frontal lobe is fully developed. We need to model appropriate interactions for students. We also need to help them make connections. Use affective statements when you are working with students. Here is an example of an affective statement. "You make me feel _____when you _____." This will encourage students to see the relationship between their actions and others. This kind of clarity really helps students develop the brain neurons. Students at this age are new at the idea of empathy, that other people have feelings and ideas that need to be considered.

Kids that enter your classroom

It may have been awhile since you have actually encountered a middle school student. You may get the wrong impression if you picture the loud group traveling together in the mall. They are not always as loud when you have them in a classroom. If you provide them with a structured environment and activities they can do, I find that I can get over 90% of students quietly engaged in tasks.

You may also be intimidated by the height of some middle schoolers. As a seventh-grade teacher and as someone slightly above average height, I usually start the year with about 5 students who are taller than I am. Some of the students I teach are shorter than my nine-year-old at home. By the end of 8th grade when I see them in the halls, at least 30% of my former students are taller than I am. Just remind yourself, they are 12 or 13. The young ladies are a mixed group, some resembling an 8-year-old with a flat chest, while others are more endowed than me and wear more makeup than I have owned in my 30 some years of life. But remember, they are still 12 or 13. Whether they are 4ft. tall or 6ft. tall, whether they wear kitty shirts or tight tops all middle schoolers are at the same stage. They all want to figure out who they are, make friends that are like them, and feel accepted.

Middle schoolers are all dealing with what it means to grow up. They are dealing with changing hormones that promote acne and high sensitivity to any words that can be sexual based. They have body odor, glasses and braces and are in the awkward transition from younger students to independent functioning high school students. Most middle schoolers can only focus on what is right in front of them, not the future or past, so they need lots of help with organization and understanding the consequences that go with the choices they make. Instead of being intimidated by the size, volume and needs of middle schoolers, just remember most of them are really insecure students who are seeking direction.

If you don't believe me that they are little kids in bigger bodies, tell the students you are playing a game and watch the over the top reaction. I have had heated games of memory that required physical intervention and students getting upset that they couldn't figure out the cheesy joke of the day. As a middle school teacher, it is important to remember they want to feel independent, but they still require structure and provisioning in order to be successful. They do not always think about consequences for their choices and they are set on hypersensitive mode so they need clear directions and expectations to feel they are being treated fairly.

Students are all unique, with varying interests, triggers and personalities. However, over the last ten years of teaching middle school I realize that the same type of students keep showing up each year. Unlike Forrest Gump's box of chocolates where you never know what you are going to get, veteran middle school teachers have a pretty good idea of personalities that will walk into their classroom. As a teacher, you learn the personalities of the students quickly and use that knowledge to differentiate the instructional needs of different classes. Some classes like to talk so they need more discussion time. Other classes are tired or work better independently. Once you see the personalities you can set up seating charts that combine different strengths of different students. All of these differences in students and the class dynamics do make middle school like a chocolate box in the way of being mostly sweet and just a little nutty.

Pro Patrick: This student is known for their athletic ability. They can be seen daily in athletic clothing with jerseys and hoodies from colleges, sports teams and private schools they want to attend. If you ask them what they want to do in the future they will immediately answer that they are going to play professional football/basketball or whatever their sport of choice. I have nothing against sports, however some of these "pro" students seem to think that athletic ability is all they need in life. They sometimes forget about following the rules, completing assignments, and being kind to others. This student feels entitled to leave class without permission, and float through middle school with all Ds and Es, except for PE of course. They don't seem to make the connection that they need to be eligible to play on that sports team, and that private schools are not interested in funding scholarships if you have behavior problems. I find that often the parents share these beliefs so connecting current behaviors with long-term goals can be difficult with these students.

What works: Try to get these athletic students on your side by building relationships. These students are often leaders so don't give them any negative attention in a large group setting, because they can derail a classroom discussion. Encourage them to participate in classroom activities where there is some sort of competition.

Patience Pushing Patty: These students take no responsibility for their actions and they always push the limits of see what they can get away with. If you redirect them, the response is *"I wasn't the only one doing something"*. Daily they teeter on the edge of getting kicked out of class or forcing you to want to write an email home. They talk when you're talking and then later have the nerve to ask for help. It appears that the word no isn't a regular word they hear in their world.

What works: Try to give yourself some space with this student because this personality can really get under your skin if you let them. Use proximity control and redirect the whole table so they don't feel targeted. Try to avoid giving them fuel for any backtalk. It's important to remember this hopefully is just a phase and they will develop into a more mature student at one point in their life.

Drama Llama Lena: These students are attention seeking, but in a moodier way. It can show up by slamming down notebooks on their table or negative comments when given a simple redirection. It also shows up as needing frequent passes to the nurse, bathroom or counseling because they need to talk to someone right now or they just aren't feeling well. If something exciting happens at lunch, they are going to have a difficult time staying focused because they thrive on the potential drama. They bother people on purpose which can escalate minor situations into situations requiring teacher involvement.

What works: To be honest, I have not perfected this personality. When they are really wound up, I will usually give them the pass they ask for because I would rather them spend five minutes in the hall then increase the drama inside the classroom. I also try on good days to build a positive rapport so that on more challenging days they don't feel like they are being picked on. Perception is their reality.

Jekyll and Hyde: This student is the student with multiple personalities depending on the environment. In class, they do their work without question, stay in their seat and talk politely. Then you get a glance of them in the hallway cussing out a friend or pushing a lonely 6th grader out of the way. Not to mention that the sub leaves a note that the student had to be picked up by security. These students make me nervous because after seeing the negative side outside the classroom I begin to question the sincerity of what I see in the classroom.

What works: I try to keep these students paired with positive influences in the classroom to keep the positive vibe going. Treat them with respect and try to get them to continue to show their work ethic and classroom etiquette by providing positive praise.

Attention Seeking Sam: The behaviors from this student can involve making loud farting sounds, answering questions without being called on, leaving a seat to visit other tables, or being late to class and arguing that they were not late. You don't need any extra information, I'm sure you have already come in contact with at least one or two of these students.

What works: As much as it pains me, I move these students close to my desk so that I can spend time catching up with them. If they feel like they get the positive attention from you they may be less likely to disturb the whole class. I have tables in my room, so I let these students sit on the side of the table by themselves so they are not bothering other students in their proximity.

Never Absent Allan: You will meet a few students who are not actively engaged in learning despite the fact that they are in school every single day. You check in with them during a class period and come back and see that they have done nothing since you last checked in on them. They spend their time in class sharpening their pencils, talking to friends, staring at the paper, and trying to use their cell phone during the class. This is often one of the classic debates: are their behaviors making it so they don't learn or is it that they can't learn what you're teaching so they show negative behaviors? I think it is probably a little of both, but either way they are a tough student to figure out.

What works: Give the students small jobs to help you in the classroom so they feel included and important. Check in with them when you can to try to give them some positive attention and get them started on learning tasks. Challenge them to have two problems done by the time you make your second round around the classroom.

Follower Frankie: These students can fit into the other categories because they mimic what other students are doing. They obsessively check on what the influencing student is doing instead of your instruction. They don't act disrespectfully, but they laugh at others inappropriate choices and seem to encourage silliness. They will often follow the lead on assignments as well, including copying other student's notes because they missed instruction.

What works: I try to compliment the student when they are working independently. I also talk to them and check in with them to see if they know what to do. Try different arrangements of where they should sit, but I don't recommend putting them next to the student they follow. This closeness can give the leader even more energy to be off-task.

Background Bella: This is the student who you may forget to mark absent because they are so quiet when they are in class. They never ask questions or talk to anyone in class. At some points they have you questioning if their vocal cords are intact. Their work is done but they are often found with a book or sketch pad when they finish work early. They might be shy, or not have friends in the class, but for whatever reason they don't participate vocally in class. In the craziness of a middle school sometimes we need to remember to be thankful for a few students who keep us sane and listen to directions.

What works: I always address these students by name at the door when possible. I want them to know they are noticed even if they choose not to talk. I also sit them with students who are calm so that when we do group work, they won't feel overwhelmed. If they have other students they seem to be friendly with, I put them together so they can be shy together.

Nosy Nate: There are some students who always have to be in the know and know everyone else's business. If you are absent from school they want to know where you were and they want to hear about any fight that may have happened on the bus or in the cafeteria. When other classmates are upset, they want to know why and what happened. It may seem like they are really caring, but most times the roots for this behavior are more about them being in the know more than the sincerity of caring for others.

What works: I try to seat these students up front where they can focus on the lesson. They will spend a lot of time observing other students instead of classroom directions if they are too far back.

Angelic Ahmir: As you go through the day, there are some students that remind you why you went into teaching. They have warmup papers out on their desk when the bell rings, they answer questions politely in class, and they work nicely with other students. They remind you that you did in fact teach the material when you grade quizzes and the class average is not encouraging.

What works: I try to provide verbal and written praise for doing a great job. I try not to put all of the difficult students with them because they shouldn't be punished for doing the right thing.

As you can see, personalities are all over the place in middle school. With the hormonal ups and downs, growth spurts, and daily changes in friend groups, students can change personalities on a daily basis. You can use your knowledge of personalities to try to put groups of students together for activities using strategically planned groups. Students working in a group can complement one another. Just know that middle school students are subject to change, and there is no such thing as a perfect seating chart. You need to think about seating charts, but don't spend hours dwelling on it, there are too many variables that change and too many unpredictable behaviors to reach perfection. Try your best with seating charts and change them as needed. A wise teacher friend once told me to remember that most of our students will turn out fine by the time they hit high school, but we are seeing them at their worst. This may not be encouraging, but remember they are not always in control of themselves and they are still figuring out these new brain connections. Try to be patient and remember you probably weren't your best self every day in middle school either. Whatever you do, remember that students are very emotional at this age, and they all need a fresh start each day. They read your verbal and non-verbal cues well, so do a really convincing job that you are glad they are here to learn.

Individual Student Needs

Middle school is, as I have mentioned, a growing time both physically and mentally. The academic abilities range greatly in middle schoolers similar to their differences in size and shape. Middle schoolers can be reading below grade level at the elementary level all the way up to high school readers. The readiness levels vary, so we need to be aware of where students are performing and how we can support them. Many of the skills that are common practice in high school like research, group projects, annotation and other skills are taught in middle school. These skills need to be explicitly taught and students need a lot of support to complete these higher-level skills. Even though we want to meet all of our students' needs, there are certain students that we really need to be aware of including students with IEPs, 504s and students learning English as a second language.

IEP: Some students come to class with what is known as an IEP or an Individual Education Plan. These students have been identified with some sort of learning disability. Based on their needs, they have a plan in place to support them in areas where they have some learning deficits. They may need extra support in reading, extra time to complete assignments, or the ability to use a calculator during math work. Every student's IEP is unique to their needs. As their teacher of record, you need to be familiar with their needs and their accommodations. Talk to teachers in the special education department about how to help students because offering supports listed in their IEP is a requirement.

504: A 504 is a different kind of learning plan for other learning impairments or physical health needs coming from Section 504 of the Rehabilitation Act. There are a wide variety of needs that are addressed in a written 504. Students with 504 could have ADD, ADHD, depression, or they could have medical needs like diabetes, sickle cell anemia, or any other medical need that requires some accommodations in the classroom. Accommodations depend on the student's needs. They often require extra time, modified assignments, preferential seating or access to medical services. Some students need bathroom breaks, extra water or whatever can make students comfortable and successful in a classroom space. Just like an IEP, you need to learn the background of your students because we are legally required to meet the needs of students in our classroom space.

English Language Learner: Sometimes you get students who are very new in this country and are just starting to learn the English language. They may be recent to the United States and have no skills in English or they could have been here for several years and still are working on learning the language. Students often can listen and speak English successfully long before they can read it and write it. Students who are listed as ESOL or ELL have individual plans that show where they are at in their readiness for tasks. Most times these students are hard workers. In order to fit in with the class they will nod their head that they understand even when they don't really understand the content or the activity. These students benefit from lots of visuals including images and videos. After I get the class started, I try to visit them directly and go over directions slowly. I try to make modified assignments whenever I can so that they have less writing and more picture cues.

The strategies that you use in class to help individual student needs will not just benefit students with individual plans, these strategies benefit everyone in the class. All students benefit from clear directions, check ins, visuals, and notes and graphic organizers. When you plan a lesson think about how you will make the content accessible for students with need first. The strategies and scaffolding that you plan will be a win-win for everyone.

Kids these days

Some of the behaviors that you see in a middle school today are likely to have you shaking your head and questioning your choice to become a middle school educator. The behaviors are not easy to deal with, but in my honest opinion it's not the kids that have changed but more the parents. Changes in parenting have led to more challenging behaviors in the classroom. In my experience, the root of many behavior problems lies in the changing role of parents and families outside of the school day. Let's explore why our students are struggling and what we as teachers can do about it.

Time Alone: Middle schoolers spend more time by themselves than they have in the past. Many students get themselves up for school in the morning and come home to an empty house in the afternoon. When they are at home, many students move into their rooms to play on their phones and video game systems. Based on parents' demanding work schedules and other responsibilities, family dinners and family time are often a thing of the past. Middle schoolers are kids, and they are not developmentally ready to take responsibility for day to day tasks such as getting ready, finishing homework, making meals, and doing laundry. If you add in all of the adult content they are exposed to on TV and social media, you can see a foundation for behavior problems. Bottom line: most middle schoolers are given more freedom than you were at the same age, and not surprisingly, they don't make the best choices with that added freedom.

Classroom Impacts: If students are used to making their own decisions all the time at home, then they're going to be more resistant to a teacher telling them what to do. From a developmental standpoint, middle schoolers need structure although they act like they don't. Make your classroom a safe space with consistent routines and expectations. Successful teachers find a way to enforce expectations without a power struggle. Phrases like "In this classroom we…" show that you have your own classroom criteria for success not necessarily connected to other classrooms or life outside of school. Also, a note of caution: students who get themselves ready for school have a higher number of absences so they often struggle to keep up with assignments.

Nutrition: Linked to what I listed above, students are often responsible for making their own food choices for breakfast, lunch and sometimes even dinner. A twelve-year-old tends to choose foods that taste good over their nutritious but less tasty counterparts. If they are fending for themselves, they look for something quick, usually meaning it comes from a package. I see students at 7:45 in the morning eating hot Cheetos and drinking soda. If I ate that, I would feel sick to my stomach, not feel full, and then get a headache due to the effects of sugar and preservatives. I would also be a basket case in the classroom. For the students who get meals provided by the school, they may get a full belly, but their school diet is high in processed foods, salt and sugar. These students get few if any fruits and vegetables in their daily diet. The lack of vitamins and minerals makes it difficult for their body to function properly or to have energy available for learning. They have no balanced diet. In addition to poor food choices, students drink Gatorade, sodas and juice all of which are full of added sugar. The amount of actual water they drink is minimal. In a nutshell, many students are dehydrated and constantly dealing with the ups and downs of a high sugar/salt diet.

Classroom Impacts: Nutrition deficits lead to behaviors ranging from students who sleep and drool on the desk all the way to those trying to stand on the desk. Students have upset stomachs, unpleasant aromas and impulsive behaviors. I believe that many of the classroom behavior struggles could be improved with simple diet changes. Sadly, you can't burn all of the vending machine snacks, but you can model healthy choices and make some recommendations. Overall, there is not much we can do here.

Sleep: Research from the National Sleep Foundation recommends that students aged 11-14 get eight to ten hours of sleep daily. After talking to many students, I have found that their sleep schedule often involves staying up until close to midnight and then dragging themselves out of bed around 6:00 to get ready for school. This is due to playing video games with friends or interrupted sleep from technology alerts and text messages. Remember that a student's chemical composition is changing making it so they don't feel tired until late at night. When students catch up on sleep on the weekends by sleeping 12 hours at a time, it throws off the body's natural circadian rhythm (the part of your body that tells us a natural wake up and sleep time). One magazine article suggests that only 10-15% of middle school students are meeting the recommended sleep goals.

Classroom Impacts: Sleep helps activate memories so when students don't get enough sleep, they can't remember what they learned the day before. They may need activators to get their brain reset on the topic. Sleep also influences mood and overtired students are more likely to be hypersensitive to comments. You say, "have a seat", but they hear, "Do it now and I hate you." While this may be a slight exaggeration, the key for adults is to be as calm as possible with students so they have less room to misconstrue the things you say.

Exercise: The NFL fully supports the play60 initiative, meaning that students are recommended to exercise at least 60 minutes a day. For the students I teach, I know they are nowhere close to that. Fewer and fewer students are involved with extracurricular activities due to lack of interest, transportation, money or all of the above. Most of my students go home and immediately plug into technology and never go outside after school. If PE is 45 minutes during the day, after the locker room time and directions students are probably only getting 25 minutes of exercise within the school day. They are missing out on natural sunlight and need an outlet for their physical energy. This affects students in many ways, but most commonly it can make they very restless and fidgety or it can make them very sedentary and sleepy from a lack of proper blood flow.

Classroom Impacts: Many students can't sit still. They use up excessive energy by kicking the desk in front of them, tapping their pencil, sharpening their pencils five times and talking non-stop. Not only are these behaviors very annoying, they also take away from learning. I try to start my class with an activator question using a two-minute timer. In those two minutes students can sharpen pencils and calm their bodies for learning. If they are still fidgety and silly, we shake up our glitter jar and breathe calmly while we watch the glitter settle. Try to be patient and give students options for movement when possible in the classroom. Let them stand up for independent work or try to add in learning stations where students move around the room for research and learning.

I believe diet, schedules and supervision, sleep and exercise all contribute to the behaviors we see in the classroom. As frustrating as it can be, it can also be a reminder that you can only work with what you are given. You cannot affect the decisions that happen outside of our 45 minutes a day. I'm not saying I agree with any of these decisions that families are making, I just want to be realistic about the challenges. I hope and pray that parents will be able to step in for their students and provide them with guidance and support in all of the areas of the middle schooler's life. However, I understand that parents are under stress financially and need to work, often at night or in mornings or both. I also understand that they want to be close with their students, which sometimes means being more like friends than a clear authority figure. Parents love their kids, and may be unaware that the choices their students make outside of school have side effects that impact learning. Rather than making parents the enemy, work with them in whatever capacity you can to help the child. Realize which factors are out of your control and implement super lessons in spite of them!

Chapter 3: The Staff at Middle School

As a middle school teacher, you will typically spend between 3.5 and 4 hours a day with students. A big part of your success will be the relationships and structures you develop in your own classroom. However, middle schools work like machines and they need all parts to be working to get the best results. It is important to understand the roles of different staff at a school, and ways to build positive relationships with staff. Other adults can be a great support when you are working in a world of 12-year-olds.

Principals You Meet

I am in my 15th year of teaching. Although I have stayed in the same school system, I have encountered a wide variety of principals in the schools where I have served. During my last seven years at the same current school, I have worked under four principals. I think a good thing to remember about principals is: don't get too attached or too upset, because their placements seem to be relatively fluid. If you can deal with the basics of how they run the school, you can do okay. If you are frustrated, wait it out for a while to see if they last or if they follow through with what they say during pre-service. I have come to see principals more like politicians. Preservice is the campaign, everything is going to be better and different. When the reality of 800 students on a daily basis sets in those promises and overwhelming initiatives start to shrink as they are just not sustainable.

As I get more years under my belt, I no longer get stressed when I hear statements like the following during pre-service:

"I expect 10 positive parent contacts a week."

"I'll be visiting classrooms weekly; this is my school and I want to see what is happening."

I don't want to give the wrong impression, principals are important. I have always strived to have a respectful professional relationship with my principals. I just realize that everyone is optimistic at the beginning, and the reality is they can't be everywhere they want to be. I remain a neutral party with my principal, or as you might say fly under the radar. I never have anything to hide in my classroom, I just focus on doing what I think is best for my students within the school guidelines without the fear of administration breathing down my neck.

Here are some of the principal personalities that I have come in contact with.

Savior

Many of the schools I have worked in are highly impacted schools with academic and behavior concerns that red flag the school. A red flag is a term used to describe schools that are not meeting district benchmarks in academic progress. I have had several instances where the school system believes that bringing in a principal from a different school system will solve all of the school's problems. I have nothing against new principals, I have worked for many. However, I am always leery of someone from another district making a smooth transition into a much larger system or a system with a different set of rules.

The last "savior" I worked for yelled all the time at kids to get out of the hallways or to be quiet in the lunchroom. He was trying to intimidate the kids into conforming. He shared military strategies as if they could easily transfer into a public middle school. It worked for a little while, until the mass of students realized there was no action behind all of the loud yelling. The meetings he ran for staff were awful, he could barely work a laptop and showed the same motivational video four times during his first year. The discipline policy was completely subjective to the student in question and how he felt about them. He didn't build relationships with staff and students, so his results really backfired. In the three years it took the school system to finally fire him, we lost 75% of our staff.

How to survive: Become friendly with the assistant principals and team leaders who are more understanding and supportive. Focus on your classroom and what you can control. Take a few more days off than you would normally to avoid a major case of teacher burnout.

My takeaway: Don't say it if you don't mean it. Students thrive on consistency. The more idle threats you say, the less students believe in you. Also, a quiet serious stare can work more wonders than a big bear yell and growl.

Bully

At the current school at which I work, I was interviewed over the summer by two Assistant Principals and my content specialist. I was hired within three hours of the interview. I was feeling great about my new position, until I was pulled into the principal's office a week later. Her first question to me was, "Did my Assistant Principal's make a good choice in hiring you?" At that point I was not sure I even had the job and I really had no idea how to answer. I felt so uncomfortable with her in the office, that I felt like I shrunk to my middle school self in trouble with the principal.

Throughout the year, I realized fear was her biggest tactic with staff and students. Students obeyed when she was in sight out of nothing more than fear. Teachers were afraid to bring discipline problems to her attention in fear of being reprimanded. When she had some after school program she wanted to run she would target teachers who she thought could help, and then make them feel pressured to take on extra responsibilities. Lucky for me, she was promoted to a central office position at the end of the year.

How to survive: Make close friends with experienced teachers in your hallway that can support you with lower level discipline problems. They will sometimes take kids to their room for a break, and give you ideas on how to solve some of the problems you are facing. Only work with administration on high level issues so you limit your interactions with the bully.

My takeaway: Treat others as you want to be treated. I never want my own students to view me in the way I viewed my former principal.

Sitting Duck

This principal came with amazing recommendations. As an assistant principal, she was active in classrooms and the community. She knew the names of all the students in the school and waited outside greeting the buses each morning. My school couldn't wait to see this positive principal in action. We soon realized that once she got the final destination job, she started taking a back seat to those little details that once made her a great vice principal. She spent more time in her office and less time in the halls, cafeteria and classroom. She utilized her vice principal to handle the discipline and other staff members to run meetings with teachers. She was the face of the school without putting in the time to be part of the school's daily operations. Luckily for her, she kept an experienced staff on board and the rest of the staff continued to make the school run efficiently despite her.

How to survive: Focus each day on doing what you think is best for students. Ask forgiveness not permission and try out new ideas or initiatives in your classroom. Instead of focusing on what the principal is not doing, focus on the freedom you have and enjoy it.

My Takeaway: Teachers have power to make a difference. The effectiveness of a school comes from all the moving parts, and you shouldn't be in a position to require administrative support daily to make or break your day.

Micromanager

Everyone has come in contact with this personality, this principal wants to be involved with everything. This principal wanted to be included on every parent email sent, she wanted access to all of our electronic lesson plans, she tried to attend every team meeting, and the list goes on. I think that the new teachers were overwhelmed with her presence, as such a stark contrast to what we had seen in the past. I however, decided to wait out the storm. I realized that the fantasy she lived in was going to come crashing down because of the reality of the strain of day to day operations and exhaustion.

I realized this type of principal really wants to establish herself as an authority. Some of my coworkers started the year meeting with her about unrealistic expectations for staff. I totally agreed with them; however, I didn't want to burn any professional bridges. School systems can be a small world and you want to make sure you leave your options open for jobs. I chose to do what was asked in a way that did not add stress to my plate. For example, when it came to online lesson plans, I would keep a Chromebook open while I was planning with my cohort and type in a line for each day as we were planning. In five minutes, I met the criteria without putting a lot of effort into something that didn't help me or my students. I added her to each parent contact email like I was asked, because I am not hiding anything. Over the course of a few months, she requested to be taken off parent emails unless we felt it was needed. As I suspected waiting out the storm was the best option.

How to survive: Play Nice! Do your best to do what is asked in a way that does not take up your valuable time. Nod your head at staff meetings and then go back to doing what is best for your classroom. Try to avoid situations where you seem to be questioning the authority of a principal who obviously fights the power struggle.

My Takeaway: Just like it was exhausting for my principal to try to be involved with every detail of the school, it is exhausting for me to try to involve myself with every detail in my classroom. I can never control every single action and choice that my students decide, so I need to take a step back and breathe when it comes to day to day dealings in my four walls.

Always Positive No Results

Most schools have some sort of positive discipline program in place which is great. However, when you are working with students there is always going to be a time where you need to have consequences in place for when students are not following rules and expectations. Meet the always positive principal. When I worked under this principal and met with him about some of my team's concerns, he would answer with statements like, "we should also think about the students who are doing great," or "what do you think you should do?" He wanted to be friendly with everyone all the time. He was kind to parents and supportive to staff. I would hear him in the hallways asking students if they wanted to go to class. Really? The result of this principal, exactly what you would expect, students walked all over him. The small number of rebellious pre-teens grew as the year went on and many school rules became optional by mid-January.

How to survive: Handle discipline problems with your own high expectations daily. Realize that you cannot solve all of the world's problems and focus on what you can control in your circle of influence (your classroom).

My takeaway: Ever since working with this principal I have increased my effort in really getting to know and focusing on students who are doing great. I write thank you notes and send positive emails and it is a satisfying part of my job. It keeps me feeling positive on days when other students are struggling. It also encourages those students to continue to do the right thing. I work on being firm and consistent with all students on procedures and behaviors from day one to avoid battles later on in the year.

Favorite Picker

A principal in my last school had been the reigning principal for 20 years in the same building. This kind of timeline in a school system the size of mine is unheard of. Teachers moved through my school every three years once they were tenured in the county. I often wondered what it was that made some teachers stay long-term and others hit the road running. In a challenging school, some teachers wanted to move to a less impacted school, and some teachers wanted to find a closer commute. However, in my second and third years it became apparent that a lot of the teacher transition had to do with favoritism. If you were in the clique, the way you were treated was much different than how others were treated.

Teachers that were well liked were moved into non-classroom positions where the schedule was pretty flexible. Other teachers were forced to move to different grade levels that they didn't want to teach as a way to encourage them to move on. Teachers who were not favored would have surprise observations on days before holiday breaks and other inconvenient times. I didn't see this treatment at first as I was in an isolated position that did not go through the same evaluation, and it really hurt staff morale once it became more visible.

How to survive: Become a sounding board for the frustration of others. Listen and share your concerns with other trusted staff members and give them feedback when they ask. Join the social committee and try to increase staff morale. If you are feeling discriminated against, decide next steps on what works best for you professionally. It's okay to think about changing schools if it's not working for you.

My takeaway: Students can see favoritism the same way staff could see it. Try to develop relationships with all students, and work to find positive things to share with all students. If students feel like they are not being treated equally, the behaviors will only go downhill from there.

I write this to share with you that I do not believe there is such a thing as a perfect principal. If you are interviewing for jobs think about whether the school is a place you can work. If the principal's requests are somewhat reasonable and the commute and class schedule is good for you then you can probably make it work. I would also look into who you will be working with as a cohort, because you will work with them daily and they may end up having more impact on your day than the principal. If the principal's pressure in the interview is leaving you in a panic it might not be the best fit for you. A principal can change the school, but they can't save it. There are a lot of other factors that determine your ability to be happy in a school, so don't count the principal as the only deciding factor in choosing a school.

Vice Principals or Other Administrators

Larger middle schools have at least one vice principal, or sometimes known as an assistant principal. I find that these individuals are the real worker bees in a middle school. They take the directive from the principal to carry out day to day operations. They open the school building, figure out class coverage, help manage the cafeteria and respond to calls to the office for assistance. As they are so involved with students on a daily basis, they are usually a great source of information for teachers who have students of concern. They may know more of the backstory or have strategies to work with students. They also can be less intimidating to talk to then the principal if you need advice or support. While they are helpful and approachable, they are also stretched thin, so decide if the situation requires them or if a content specialist or counselor may be able to assist you. They usually already have a full plate so try to spread the love when it comes to getting the support you need. Also, make sure to share your appreciation to them. Smiles, thank you notes, or help in the lunchroom are all free ways to show you appreciate what they do each day. That way next time you need a student removed from your class; you will get an understanding response.

Co-teachers and Co-Planners

Content Alike Teachers

Many times, if you interview at a middle school, other content alike teachers will sit in on an interview. I think the idea of figuring out who you will be working with should be a deciding factor in a job interview. I plan with what is called my cohort (grade and subject alike) teachers three times a week. Our working relationship impacts my day in a far more substantial way than the principal at my school. Try to get a read on them at the interview: do they seem knowledgeable but flexible. You really don't want to work with someone who is still using copies of worksheets that were originally copied on a ditto machine around 1985. Once you get your job, establish some ground rules with how you want to work with the other teacher. Who will be in charge of what? Talk to your content specialist to see exactly what needs to be the same, and where you have room to be an individual. For example, at my school the rule is that all of our quizzes have to be the same and the same point value in the gradebook. We can change how we teach the material as long as they can arrive at the same understanding. This is an equitable practice to make sure all students get exposure to the same content. If you work smarter with your cohort, it saves you from hours of being too independent and working harder.

Not only can other teachers help lessen your burden of lesson planning, but they can also be a listening voice for you when you are having trouble with student behavior. They can support you with strategies when students are not getting the content. Try to build this relationship so that you can count on one another. For example, if you have a good working relationship, they would be more likely to help make sub plans for you on an emergency sick day.

Co-Teachers

Most public schools have at least one or two sections where you will have a co-teacher in the room. Typically, those teachers are there to support ESOL students, students with IEPs, students with 504 plans or other health needs. These co-teachers can be a huge lifeline, so make sure that you start the year ensuring that every student knows their name and that you are both teachers. You want to give them meaningful tasks in the classroom and involve them in any teaching they feel comfortable with. Ask them how they want to be involved at the beginning so they feel like they are part of the class. Put their name on the door for the section they teach with you. Ask them for their input on seating charts or other things that involve working with students. Seeking their opinions is a way to make sure they are valued, and they might see things that you miss. A different perspective might be just what you need to tackle a challenge in the classroom.

Team Support

Even though I have taught elementary and middle school, I think one of the reasons I have enjoyed middle school more is the team model that a lot of middle schools put in place. A team typically consists of all or most of the teachers at a specific grade level. At my school, the core grade level team has a shared period off where we can meet while the students are in PE or electives. We meet twice during the week. I like knowing I am not the only one teaching a student, and by wrapping around the students with all of our expertise and strategies we are able to make real progress with students that we have concerns about. Since other teachers teach the same students, they can be an invaluable support when it comes to finding new ideas to try or just to listen when you have lost your patience and your mind. Having other middle school teachers who face the same struggles prevents me from feeling alone.

At my school we meet as a team at least once a week. During that meeting we find out what is going on within the school through leadership updates, testing schedules, field trips and other business items. We use a team as a way to keep everyone informed on what is going on in the building. After we cover the business end, we turn our focus to student growth. We talk about student academics and behaviors. We schedule parent conferences for students and discuss what is working in one classroom that could possibly be tried in another classroom to produce the same positive results. During various points in the quarter we call students in for grade checkups where we meet with them to develop plans for improving their grades in various subjects. This helps those students who are needing support with executive functioning (planning ahead, staying organized, and making improvements). My absolute favorite reason I love my team is when we call students in for a conference. Four to five teachers and hopefully the counselor will sit and talk to a student at one time. This slightly intimidating conference shows the student that we mean business and gives the students the chance to see that all of the staff cares about them enough that we took our time to meet with just them.

Team members can be amazing support for you at school. They can sympathize with you, support you, and give you chocolate when needed. If you are lucky enough to teach in a school with a grade level team, establish a level of trust with them and work together to see great results with students. Most of my close friends at school develop from my team.

Building Services, Secretaries and Other Support Staff

Some of my mom's biggest teaching advice was to make friends with the secretaries and the building services in your building. This has proved to be some of the soundest advice I have received for many reasons. First, both the secretaries and building services work long hours to make the school run and they often get very little recognition. A smile and a thank you can go a long way in making their day. Also, I am a science teacher and I have more mess than most classrooms. I am always kind to building services staff and they are kind to me by bringing me extra trash cans, helping me fix sink faucets and broken electrical plugs. The secretaries are the unsung heroes of the school. They know everything, so you want to be on their good list. They are useful if you want to know about any school happenings, if you need to take leave, or order materials.

Here are some ways I make sure to keep in good terms with these supporting staff. I try to write them each individual thank you notes throughout the year for something specific they help me with. Around the holidays, I try to leave some sweet treats for them to enjoy in their office space. Small acts of kindness go a long way!

Chapter 4. Taming the Classroom: Ideas that Work for students

Me and my classroom

I have already mentioned that I go against the typical picture of a classroom teacher who has neatly applied makeup, a great fitting pencil skirt and a classroom that sparkles clean. I wear elastic waist band pants 90% of the time, I never wear any makeup, and sometimes I even forget to brush my teeth in the morning because I'm so rushed. My rushed physical appearance sometimes reflects my classroom where I like to pile any papers without a logical home on the bottomless pit of my desk. Even though I appear rushed and frantic, my classroom runs very smoothly. I'm a classic don't judge a book by its cover.

Middle school classrooms can be orderly, productive and well managed. You the teacher have to construct a classroom with provisions, organizations and teaching practices that build positive relationships with students. You need systems, structures and consistency. You need to design a classroom that works for YOU!

Operation Organization

How can a completely disorganized personality manage a classroom with 150 students? Since I knew this was a challenge for me, I was disciplined in learning organization. I studied, taking graduate school classes on how to be organized, and watching other teachers who were masters at organizing. I tried new systems each quarter and school year until I came up with the recipe that worked for me in my own space. The key here, I found what worked for *me* in *my* space. Many of the systems that I tried shamelessly to copy from coworkers did not work for me and they left me with increased levels of stress.

Why is being organized so important? I didn't understand the depth of this until I took a graduate school class on classroom organization last fall. Here are the reasons teachers need to be organized, and it has very little to do with observations or what other teachers feel.

It's About You
1. If you walk into a classroom where you have all the papers for the day, a place for student work, a lesson plan, and materials out that you need for the day you will feel more prepared.
2. If you are prepared then you can use your planning time to accomplish new things and get prepared for the next day instead of rushing to the copier to make up for your lack of provisioning.
3. If you the teacher feels prepared, you are less stressed.
4. If you are less stressed, then you are better able to handle the hormonal, immature, unpredictable behaviors that will enter your classroom.
5. Smooth classroom systems help students know what to do when you have a substitute. If students know what is expected your classroom will be in better shape when you return and students don't have the excuse that they didn't

know where to turn work in or what you expect from them.

Translation: Organization is about feeling good mentally to start your day. You feel in control, it's good for your brain and for your physical body stress. It gives you mental energy to attack the to-do list of 200 other things you need to get done today. If you see teachers who aren't pulling their hair out and actually eat lunch in more than 2 minutes it's because they are organized and prepared for the day, maybe even for the week. You want to train yourself to be organized so you can get ahead instead of digging yourself out of plies of unending paperwork.

It's About Your Students

1. You set the vibe for the classroom, if you are stressed, they feel that stress too and it puts a sour edgy vibe to your classroom.
2. If you are unprepared, students will use the time you take to find their papers to do what they want to do. Warning, what students want to do is: talk to friends, play basketball with old papers, physically bother another student, say something inappropriate, get on their phone etc. The majority of middle school students do not want to do what you want them to do. If you are organized, they don't have time to do these things, they only have time for completing the work you assign.
3. Students who are busy are easier to manage. The best compliment students can give me is, "*We never have any free time in your class*".
4. In the same way that a disorganized classroom can be stressful for you as a teacher, it can be stressful for students. An organized classroom is reassuring! Students are calmer, ready to learn and more likely to be successful.
5. If you have clean counters and clean tables, you model for students that we respect this place and we make an effort to keep it clean. Part of keeping a classroom organized is taking the time to teach students how to do their part. I show my students how to borrow and return materials, where to turn in work and how their tables should look when they leave. Never do something in the classroom

57

that your students can do for you. Use your time for other things instead of cleaning up after students.

Setting up your classroom

Did you know that so much of your classroom management starts before the students even enter the classroom? The key here is what works for students is using systems! If you have no idea how to set up a classroom, you should start by taking a tour of experienced teachers' classroom space. Start by looking at your subject alike teacher's classroom, and then travel to other members of your grade level team. Take a notebook with you and ask questions as you visit. Take note of their table arrangements, ask them how they collect student work, how do they keep track of materials and assignments. The more you ask, the more you know. It helps to talk to multiple teachers because then you have ideas to use that you can adapt for yourself.

I can always spot an inexperienced teacher during pre-service week because they spend over a day of that precious week on a beautiful bulletin board straight from Pinterest. I feel concerned for these new naïve teachers because they think they are so prepared. As a veteran teacher, my theory on decorating my classroom and bulletin boards is, less is more. I have one content wall where I change posters every quarter to match our curriculum and one place for student recognition. I also have a "ME" area where I show pictures of my family, vacations and outside interests. Students like to know the "human" side of their teachers so I make the pictures accessible to them instead of having them hover over my desk area to see photos. Everything else in my classroom stays the same year to year.

Fight the urge for the perfect bulletin board and spend time doing more important things:

- Figure out how to arrange student desks/tables so every student can see the board
- Figure out if you want individual or groups of students sitting together
- Make sure you can move to every part of your classroom to access every student

- Post the emergency exit plan for fire drills or any drill that requires you to leave the classroom
- Set up an area for handing out student papers and student materials
- Set up an area to collect student papers and student materials
- Post classroom expectations
- Figure out how you want students to come in and out of the classroom and what you want them to do during class activities
- If you have access to technology (tablets, Chromebooks, laptops) figure out how you want to store the technology and use it with students
- Make seating charts so students know where to sit when they arrive
- Plan the week ahead for lessons so students will have something to do when they arrive

If you do not plan for all of these things, you are giving students too much freedom in the classroom. The classroom is your space and when you are proactive in the way you set up your classroom you eliminate issues before they arise.

Problems caused by ineffective classroom setups:

Students seats that are packed in too tight have a tendency to get pushy with one another as they bump each other trying to get to their seats.

You can't access some student desks so they are basically given freedom to do what they want because you can't use proximity control.

You don't have a plan to collect papers, so student work ends up getting lost. Lost papers lead to distrust and frustration between you and your students.

You don't have a plan on how to clean up a hands-on activity (card sorts, manipulatives) so 10 sets of materials are left all over tables and the floor as the bell rings. You cannot do this activity with your next class because you did not provision time for students to clean up.

Big Idea: Set yourself up for success by planning with the end in mind. Physically arrange your classroom in a way that is conducive to learning. Then, plan for what the students will do to access the learning while they are in your space. Both of these ideas are going to take you much further than that beautiful 3D bulletin board.

Organizing Lesson Plans and Student Papers

Teaching can be scary because so much of your success is based on YOU! It is very easy for struggling teachers to say it was because of the behaviors of the students, unsupportive parents or too many preps. Yes, these areas can cause challenges, but most of the success in the classroom comes from your ability to provision, plan and execute quality instruction. You determine your own success. If you want to get in better shape, you can't blame the gym hours or your lack of support from your spouse, or your DNA. You choose what you eat and your activity, so your success is largely dependent on you. You can be successful in the classroom the same way you can make healthy life choices.

If the weight of teaching success is weighing on your shoulders, how do you attack it? First, you follow the clues that I provided to set up your classroom as an awesome learning zone. Then you take step two, plan for instruction.

Lesson Plans

Teachers need to write lesson plans, not those terrible four-page lessons plans you did as an undergraduate, but some written documentation of what you are going to do. Some schools have required formats that you have to follow, but if your school does not have a required form don't think you can just get out of doing it. I am old school so I go out and buy an academic planner that I write my plans in each day. Lesson plans should cover a variety of questions, what is the objective (what do students need to learn), what is the agenda (how will the students learn), and evaluation (how will I know the students learned). If you keep these three questions in your mind you are on your way to success.

Keep Good Records

If you write lesson plans on an old napkin, they won't be helpful because you will lose them before you use them. Write them on paper or electronically which ever you want and put them in a meaningful location where you can access them. Master teachers become master teachers because they save lesson plans and they make notes and edit them so they are able to be better prepared to deliver that topic again in the future. I don't reinvent the wheel; I tweak lessons that were pretty good and I get rid of lessons that turned into a hot mess. For example, one time the curriculum suggested a lab where students use beads and pipe cleaners to show chemical reactions. It took forever to set up the lab, the beads kept dropping or were turned into projectiles. I had to completely reteach that lesson and I was slipping on beads for days as an after effect. My memory fails me often, so if I didn't keep a record of my plans, I would repeat the bead disaster over again before remembering how awful it was. I learn and grow and improve from reflecting on my own documentation. Even if you are lucky enough to have a district that provides a basic curriculum you still have to make it your own before bringing it to the classroom.

Different levels of planning

Lesson plans come in all different levels. There are basic overviews of what you want to get done in the unit, check points of how you assess student learnings, and day to day plans that vary on topics. Some of these you may plan with a cohort (subject alike teacher) and some you do on your own. The more time you spend planning the better your lessons will be. I talk to myself as I plan, sometimes even out loud. I ask myself a lot of questions when it comes to planning. The more questions you ask yourself and your cohort, the clearer your lesson is and the easier it is to share with students. If you just scrape the surface of lesson planning and print off a worksheet you found on the internet, you will be spending the whole class period answering questions about what to do and how to find the information. After doing that over and over for each class you will have a very hoarse voice and may consider pulling your own hair out. These types of disasters cause you to use your precious spare change on the overpriced candy machine in the staff lounge, and you will think teaching is just too hard. Save yourself the empty calories and stress by putting more thought into what you are teaching and how you will deliver information to students.

Just remember the success of your classroom depends on you. Be honest, are your students really awful or did you not adequately prepare them to be successful? Cricket! Cricket!

Start talking to yourself like I do, I swear it keeps me sane.

Helpful Hint: If you are lucky enough to have a guided curriculum, don't think you have to use it exactly as it is written. If you look over an activity and you are bored reading it, then it will certainly be boring to your students. See if you can take steps to "de-borify" it with group work or a fun summarizer. If you use your creative energy to tweak it and it's still boring, it may be time to look for an alternative assignment to achieve the same objective. I find that my suggested curriculum provides six-page labs for students. I find this length inappropriate for middle school students not to mention very environmentally unfriendly. You might be able to do the same lab and reduce the arrangement and questions to make it work better for your classroom.

Questions to consider when lesson planning:

Long-term planning questions
- What are the big ideas in this unit?
- What big projects or assessments take place throughout the unit?

Short Term Planning
- What topics will we cover this week?
- Where should we be at by the end of the week?
- How will we know if students have learned the material by the end of the week?

Daily Planning: (This is where you need to work through this on your own to make sure whatever you planned with other teachers works in your space!)

- What is the objective for the students learning today?
- What do I want them to do when they come into the classroom? (Activator, read the background of notes)
- What learning materials do I need to give to students?
- How will they get this information? (Reading, online research, stations, independent work, group work?)
- How long will they need to do this activity?
- How will I introduce the topic so students can do their work?
- How will I be involved in student learning? (Pulling groups, circling the classroom)
- How are students supposed to ask me for help? (Do they need to stay in their seats, come see you, what is the expectation?)

Whatever you plan for, you also need to convey that expectation and plan to students. Most students will do what they are asked if you are clear and reasonable with expectations. Share with students the answers to these questions before they get started on assignments.

Structure is Key

Middle schoolers love to act like they don't need help or structure. They love to give you an eye roll when you make them repeat instructions. They may act like they hate structure and want freedom, but most of the time they really do well with a structured lesson and they are more productive academically when they have guidance.

Here are some examples of places the classroom where structure is needed.

1. Students need routines in the classroom. They need something to do throughout the class time, starting before the bell rings. If you wait until the bell rings to start instruction, you miss up to three minutes a day because it takes that long to get them settled and started. I prefer to start them with a question on the board or a warmup. Every day I set the timer for two minutes. When that timer goes off, they need to have an answer to the warmup, sharpened their pencil, and get in their assigned seat. I go over this routine for the first two weeks of school so that it becomes a habit. If students are talking when the timer goes off, I give one class reminder and then move directly to the death stare targeted at said talker. Students will nudge their neighbors to get them to quiet down because the stare is that good. This structure starts the class in a way that is quiet and calm so students are ready to learn.

2. Students need clear expectations for both behaviors and academic work. Teenagers resort to the unfair game and sharing your expectations helps prevent them from pulling the unfair card. Are they working alone, with a partner or with a group? Are they allowed to get out of their seat? How do they ask for help? All of these expectations were part of your ingenious planning so all you do is share them with students to create a fair level playing field. Make sure you tell them what is expected for the specific assignment such as using three sources or highlighting the original text. When you

provide these expectations, it creates a positive work environment and it makes a classroom that is much easier to manage.

3. Students need to know where or how to turn in assignments. I suggest making the process of turning in work as part of the student's job. I don't need to accept the responsibility for making sure their work is in the right place. I use simple plastic drawers listed by class period. All work goes there anytime I collect work. It's a structure, it's predictable, it's fair and it works. Students get confused if one day they leave work on the table, one day they use a folder and one day you collect it at the door. Consistency in structure makes students feel safe and in control.

Side Note: Structure does not mean you do the same thing every day for 180 boring days. Structure means that you start the class the same way, and provide details about how the class will run for the day. You always collect work the same way and have ways to communicate with students throughout the classroom. You should include variety in classroom activities. Variety keeps students interested and also helps reach students with different learning styles.

Helping students stay organized

Most students who have failing grades in middle school fall into one of two categories:

Category 1: Students who miss so much school they cannot stay caught up on class assignments

Category 2: Students who are so unorganized that they lose assignments ALL THE TIME

So how do we help these students? Obviously as teachers we feel the pressure from the administration to make sure students have multiple opportunities to show what they know. I do the best I can to help students with frequent absences catch up. I excuse some assignments that were extra review, practice and non-essential. Besides a little extra boost, I can't make students come to school so I have to remember it is out of my control. I turn their names over to counseling, because I can only really focus on things inside my classroom.

I focus my energy on those category 2 students. You know what they look like. They have a two-inch binder with 234 papers in the front pocket. They never have a pencil even though they had one in 1st period. They leave a trail of papers from quarter 1 in the middle of March. I describe this student and you can picture them walking into your room. I actually feel the hairs on my neck stand up when I picture this type of student. How can we help them stay organized?

Tips that help all students:
- Have directions on the board, written on the paper and share them verbally so students can have multiple ways to access important information
- Collect papers in a timely manner so students don't lose papers

- Give students a minute at the end of class to file papers, put away their pencil and organize themselves before they transition to another class
- Have a system for how papers are collected that is consistent throughout the school year
- Show a picture on the board or in your hand if you need to have them find a paper that is already in their notebook
- Have a system for borrowing and returning pencils so that students can work on classwork
- Hole punch papers for students that you want them to keep in their notebook, encourage other teachers to do this also

Tips that support THAT unorganized student:
- Invite them in one day at lunch to sit down and talk about how to organize, some students don't have the executive functioning skill and they don't know how to get started
- Tell them that the front pocket of a binder is called a NO-ZONE meaning no papers go there. Every paper needs to be in an appropriate folder or divider or recycling bin
- Throw away papers with them that you know they don't need
- Make sure they have a pencil pouch that fits into the rings of the binder
- Have an organized student help them on a day you have extra time
- Check in with them once a week and give them a whole bunch of compliments if they are working to maintain staying organized
- Collect all of their papers for you each day. I have one or two students in each class that I will not let them take papers even when they are not done. I hold them in a folder and give them back to the student the next day because otherwise I am going to kill a few more trees and the students will be more behind each day when they have to start over
- Give them some grace and realize they are 12 and they will grow out of it as you give them their 3rd copy of the project you assigned

Helpful Hint: There are always going to be disorganized students. We are not going to be able to "save" them. We can offer strategies to help students help themselves. They need to focus on being organized and prepared for their classes, all we can do is provide some guidance on how to do it.

Involving students in keeping the classroom organized

Students in general can be as lazy as we let them be. Let's face it, adults are as lazy as they are allowed to be, so teenagers are no different. Students need to be taught directly how to complete all of the routines in your classroom. Remember that they travel to seven different learning spaces in a day and when the bell rings their brain is programmed to leave and get onto the fun of the hallways. If you don't teach them how to keep your classroom organized, they won't keep it clean. If you see other organized classrooms don't assume witchcraft or superpowers, assume that the teacher took the time to directly teach them the expectations for handling materials and cleaning the class BEFORE the bell.

Simple tips for organization in the classroom:
1. Don't do anything that a student can do for you. Save your time for other tasks. Some students love to help. Here is what I have students do in my classroom: sharpen pencils at the end of the day that I lend to students, undo folders with the articles we used in class, make sure all Chromebooks are plugged into the cart. Since I am a science teacher, I also have all of the lab materials to deal with. Students will offer to clean test tubes, stack baskets and otherwise clean up after labs and I always say YES please! If I did these things it would take up a good portion of my planning, I would rather use that time to set up for tomorrow.
2. Think about how long you need to clean up when you plan out your lesson and stop the lesson at the appropriate time. You should be cleaned up before the bell.
3. Practice cleaning up with students. Make it fun. Can we do it faster? Which table is cleaned up first? Students in middle school are very competitive, use it to your advantage.

4. Don't let students leave until your classroom is the way you want it. Start this at the beginning of the year and they will develop the habit of keeping clean and saving you unneeded stress.

Classroom Management

Most people who are terrified of teaching middle school don't want to hear about lesson plans and the many benefits of teaching middle school, they are only picturing themselves in front of a class of 30 hormonal predators ready to feast on them as the new naive prey. This is really an illusion; they are not as scary as they look. They are also only as scary as you let them be.

I wish I had some super cool strategy I could share with you that would reveal my classroom management superpowers, but the reality is my success comes from the provisioning I put in place to avoid problems before they happen. I physically arrange my classroom seats, seating charts, lessons and activities to keep students engaged in learning. My number one truth for middle school education is that busy students make better behaved students. In order to be busy, students need structure, expectations, and work they can be successful with. In order to stay busy, learning tasks must be engaging and interesting. My classroom management recipe is effective planning, classroom structures and holding students to high expectations.

One additional tip I have is, make sure students are engaged with tasks they can be successful with. If you give a student a 10-page article about pollinators to read and a follow up paper with questions without text features, directions and strategies then you will have chaos in less than 5 minutes. Imagine the difference if you start class by asking, "How do you feel about bees? Are they really important?" Discuss the topic with the class to pique their interest and activate prior knowledge. If you add in a two-minute video highlighting that we would have no fruits, vegetables, or clothes without bees, then you make a personal connection. Tell them to answer specific questions and annotate each of the 3 pages (not 10) of the article and soon you will have the majority of the class peacefully working with minor need to redirect. Effective management is setting students up for success and modeling what you expect for students for both their behaviors and their academics. This type of planning will work for the majority of the class, but there will always be students who require more interventions to help them to be successful.

Build Genuine Relationships

Building relationships is one of the new power phrases in education, and for some reason people are acting like this is a new idea. Relationships help you help students, and relationships help students help you. Some students are quick to judge you based on the differences they see between you and them. Students set up barriers because you are so old, so white, so tall, so rich or whatever walls they build in their minds. In order to break down those walls you need to be genuine in your efforts to build relationships with all students.

The first way to build relationships is to be open about who you are as a human being outside of the classroom walls. Students in middle school are very nosey, so I'm not suggesting you share all the contents of your phone photos and interesting adult weekend activities. I am saying within reason help students see you as more than an authority standing in front of the class. I talk about my children, my dogs, movies I like to watch. I also ask them for movie and book suggestions. These are great ways to start building some common ground. My son loves baseball so it's really easy for me to chat it up with a quiet student wearing a Washington Nationals sweatshirt. Once you open up about yourself, students will more likely open up about themselves. Look for ways to connect with students.

Start at the beginning of the year to build relationships and then continue to cultivate it in a natural progression throughout the year. I like to choose days where I leave five minutes at the end of class to ask some four corner questions. I ask a question, give four choices, and the students move to the corner that fits their interest. Some questions that are fun to ask students are: what superhero do you like best, what kinds of snack foods do you like, what is the worst part about school. If you leave questions that are surface level then students will feel more comfortable building on those questions later on. It makes nice connections among peers and helps you understand students better. I use this four corners game later on as review games or just for fun brain breaks.

Another way to build a relationship with students is to give them surveys at the beginning of the year. It takes a while to learn about 150 students so a quick survey can be an easy way to start.

Here are some questions I include on student surveys.

Name _____

1. Phonetic spelling of their name. I tell them to capitalize the sounds that are strong and leave out letters you can't hear. My last name is Burrbridge, so I show them it would be BURR-Brige. Students come from all over the world and they hate it when you mispronounce their names.
2. What they like about my subject
3. What they don't like about my subject
4. How do they prefer to work: INDIVIDUAL PARTNERS GROUPS
5. How they like to be recognized for great work
6. VERBAL PRAISE POSITIVE NOTE POSITIVE EMAIL HOME
7. Random fun questions like favorite Disney Character and favorite superhero
8. Dream vacation (No Limits)

I greet students at the door and address them by name as they enter my classroom. They know that they are seen because I addressed them as an individual. This also allows me to start my classroom management before class time starts.

Another way I build relationships with students is by using best practices in my teaching. I don't talk over students; I visit them at their desks each day. I hold them accountable for their learning and their behaviors. You may think you are encouraging kids by not being too hard on them, but many students have told me over the years that they know a certain teacher doesn't care about them because they don't make them work. Students are often looking for boundaries in the classroom, so establishing clear consistent boundaries for students makes them feel safe and that establishes positive relationships. I keep a jar of popsicle sticks with numbers that match a number for each student on my attendance list. I call on students when they least expect it. Students know they have to be engaged in learning, and that helps build our working relationship. I also build relationships by making our classroom a positive place to learn and by giving students a fresh start each day so every day all students have the chance to learn.

Once you have established positive relationships with students you will be able to help them learn more. When they feel more successful, they will listen to your requests. For example, if you know that a student struggles with reading then you can visit them and read directions to them individually. They know you care about them, and then they work harder to do better. Later if you ask the student to stop talking and follow directions, they will be more likely to comply because they know you care about them. If you give a shy student a warning that you are going to ask them to answer a question in a few minutes, you give them time to prepare and they will be more likely to have an answer rather than looking like a deer in headlights. They try because they know you care about them and you made them comfortable in front of the class.

Student Relationship Example

This year in my class I have a student we will call Chris. Chris received all D's and E's during his previous school year. He has a 504 plan for ADHD and has many impulsive behaviors. During the month of September he disrupts my class daily, and when he is redirected he loudly responds with comments like, *"I was working,"* or *"This class is so lame."* He gets lots of peer attention for his comments. He completes very little work and started to show the same behaviors he showed last year. I have him for 1st period and he is showing up late to class even though he has been in the building with plenty of time to get to class. Finally, I email home and tell Mom he really isn't showing his potential and that I am requesting that he come in for lunch help for at least two days to get caught up so we can get back on track. Chris reluctantly comes in for what he is calling "Pure Torture." We talk about his older brother who I taught years before and his new little brother I didn't know he has. He tells me he wants a dog and asks to see pictures of my dog. I bring up the gradebook to show him all of his grades and we talk about what we can do to improve the grades. He asks if he can come in tomorrow at lunch to get help with his cell project. He comes in and completes the cell project and gets an A on it. The A on a big project brings his class grade up to a C. We reach a turning point and he starts to come to class on time. I give him gentle reminders to stay on task because I remind him that I want him to be successful. I send mom a positive email when I see changes in the classroom. She responds to my email that she never gets positive emails. Later on in the school year, I get one of my favorite comments from Chris. He comes in early to class one day and hugs me awkwardly. After his awkward side hug, he tells me I used to be his 6th favorite teacher out of 7, but now I am his number 2 favorite teacher. Also, he tells me that my jokes are terrible. In his ADHD impulsive way, I know he is speaking right from the heart. We have made a connection. He is proud of what he has accomplished and he knows I support him.

Now, I can't approach every student the way I approached Chris, but I don't have to. The large majority (around 85%) of the students I teach are content to work in a positive classroom where there are clear expectations. If I call them by name or ask about their day, I can connect with them. For the students who disrupt your class or don't engage in learning, try to be creative and look for ways to show them you care. The students who need the most love and support often have the most challenging ways of showing it. Try to be an adult they can depend on.

Never talk over students

I start setting the tone on the first day of school that it's quiet when I talk. If you start talking over students, you will do it all year and you will end up losing your voice trying to talk over more and more students as the year goes on. I tell students that in our classroom we respect each other and one way we do that is by listening to each other. In my space I teach the students that when the timer goes off, conversation stops. We practice this every day, like three to four times a class period until they get it. Then a week later some kids forget and I wait them out and start physically walking towards them to indicate I need their attention. This drill and practice is so important to me because if you talk over students two major problems arise. Your students and you are not building a respectful working relationship together. Some students cannot hear directions which will lead to more problems when students need to start independent work. You will answer the same questions 20 times and your voice will be hoarse after the lesson. And then because its middle school you will have to repeat that torture of a strained voice through four more classes.

Be the Calm in the Storm

Let's face it, sometimes middle school students are known for their impulsivity and lack of filters. It can be irritating, destructive to a lesson, and sometimes hilarious. Remember that middle school brains are governed by the emotional amygdala and not always the logical, thoughtful frontal cortex of the brain. All you can do is to be the calm in the presence of their mental, physical, and emotional storms. I am not a calm person, in fact my close family and friends used to refer to the part in my hair as the "Heathometer" and they would judge just how angry I was by the increasing red levels filling my hairline. My natural state is to be easy to anger and quick to tell you why I'm right. Years of teaching and parenting my own kids has taught me ways to be calm.

How to be calm before students arrive:
- Drink lots of water and eat a healthy breakfast so you are not getting some hangry actions going on
- Practice gratitude inside and outside of the school building
- Plan out your lessons in detail for a smooth delivery
- Anticipate problems that may occur so you're not put on the spot
- Post pictures, quotes and things that make you happy all over your classroom so you can go to your happy place when challenges arrive
- Meet students at the door to get a read on students and shut down some of the silliness

How to be calm in the moment:
- Ignore behaviors that are not impacting the instruction of the whole group
- Take deep breaths (at least three)
- Wait a few seconds to respond to something that triggers your frustrated emotions
- React with as few as words as necessary

How to be calm afterwards:

- Take a walk around the classroom before visiting the student you need to address
- Talk to the student after you have gotten the class back on track

Think About it: No matter what the student does or says in your classroom, the situation can be handled in a variety of ways. Your job as the paid professional is to try to keep your eye on the prize (students are learning in a safe and positive environment). Use whatever training, mantras, and self-control you can to take the high road and rise above the emotions from a student. Be the calm!

If I dig back in my memory files, I could probably write a book about things that have happened in my own classroom that turned an emotional trigger for me to get angry. I am not superhuman, when students say and do things my inner monologue is going at full speed. I feel like the classic cartoons with the angels and devils sitting on either shoulder telling me how to proceed. I try to listen to the angel, but I have at times listened to the devil on my other shoulder. The angel is calm, while the devil is my inner self and my own emotions of pride. Experience has taught me that listening to my anger has never improved things in my classroom, or with the student in question. Even if I feel that temporary satisfaction of winning against a student, no one really wins.

Learn from my mistakes and look at this small sampling of some situations that may happen and a way to keep calm:

1. You tell a student that you need them to sit in their assigned seat. They tell you they hate this class.

CALM RESPONSE: I'm sorry you feel that way. I want you to sit where I think you will be most successful.

WHAT MY INNER SELF IS SAYING: *"I hate that I tell you every day to have a seat. I'm unhappy that you are disrupting my class. Are they still doing schedule changes?"*

2. Two students seem frustrated at one another although they are usually friends. One student gets out of his seat and physically pushes the other student.

CALM RESPONSE: (Depending on the severity of the pushing. If a student is in danger, someone obviously needs to be removed.) Walk between the students and just see if your presence can redirect them.

WHAT MY INNER SELF IS SAYING: *"I don't have time for this. I wasn't hired to babysit."*

3. You ask a student to stop talking while you explain the directions to the class. They respond that you always pick on them when other people are talking too.

CALM RESPONSE: Wait time, then a class reminder that you will wait until everyone can hear to get started. Deep breaths and more wait time.

WHAT MY INNER SELF IS SAYING: *"Of course I'm talking to you because you are always talking, and you are a huge pain."*

4. You have a student that comes in late without a pass and says they were not late.

CALM RESPONSE: Record the tardy on the tardy log and do not address the student or address them later on in the class period.

WHAT MY INNER SELF IS SAYING: *"Obviously you were late, are you calling me an idiot that I didn't hear the bell. Stop playing in the halls and then coming in here with another attention seeking behavior. Just sit down and be quiet."*

5. A student is playing a game on a Chromebook instead of doing the class assignment. They tell you it's already done even though you can see from your screen it has not even been opened.

CALM RESPONSE: Okay, can we just check together that the assignment is done. It didn't show up in my inbox to grade.

WHAT MY INNER SELF IS SAYING: *"You never even looked at it. No wonder you didn't have any idea how to do the last assessment."*

I'm being honest by saying that my inner self struggles. I feel angry and frustrated by some of the choices that students make in the classroom. One of the things that has helped me project a calmer outside appearance is one of my coworker's key phrases, quit taking it personally. I stole it from her with her permission because it is so helpful in working with teenagers.

Quit taking it personally

Remember that whole part about the teenage brain. Remember how they are driven by their amygdala which is emotional that doesn't always connect to their frontal lobe where they think about logical reasoning and consequences. Sometimes the thing they do is really more of a knee jerk reaction and most times it has nothing to do with you. You may think you are letting them off too easy if you don't go all HULK on their class outburst, but what you are really doing is modeling grace, forgiveness and control.

True confession: I have days where I get mad at students about things that have nothing to do with them.

Here is a sample infuriating morning at my house:
I overslept because I was feeling anxious last night and didn't get quality sleep. My two kids are being turtles in the morning and wanting to talk my ear off about the new Descendants movie instead of eating their breakfast. We spend five minutes looking for the media center book to avoid a major Monday morning breakdown when we should have already left the house. Of course, I'm late for work, I didn't finish my coffee and my power strip in my room won't turn on so I can't use my computer or my smartboard.

You may think I'm exaggerating but I have had that exact morning or something similar happen ten or more times this school year. Those mornings I'm edgy and more likely to snap at students. Luckily, I have evolved from my teenage self and I am able to be mindful and take some deep breaths and calm myself before going into teacher mode. If I am still feeling stressed when they enter my classroom, I usually give them a little insight to how I am feeling. They usually find it funny, and it gives them a little fair warning that I am not in the mood. My brain is able to compartmentalize and somewhat move away from the stress in my home life when I put myself in teacher mode. I wouldn't be able to do that as my 13-year-old self. I can remember being short tempered and talking back to some of my own middle school teachers when I felt overwhelmed.

Students come to class with outside baggage that has nothing to do with you and lash out unexpectedly in class. They fight with parents, miss the bus, fail a test, or have an all-out social media war going on. All of these things are floating through their brain and body when you are trying to get them excited about plant and animal cells. Middle school students cannot always compartmentalize their troubles. I am not saying that you excuse inappropriate behaviors, I'm saying deal with it in a more appropriate way.

Don't let a student calling out deter the learning of the whole class. Don't go home angry because a twelve-year-old says you are mean. Don't lose your cool because a thirteen-year-old skips your class and now you have to take extra time to deal with it. It's not about you, it's about them and the impulsive childish behaviors that they show because they are children. They are still developing kids trapped in an oversized awkward body.

One of the craziest things for me about teaching middle school is that I have gone home from work fuming about a particular student's choices in the classroom. I have vented to my mom, a coworker and my husband. I come in the next day still having a chip on my shoulder about it and they come in and say, *"Hello, I finished my project. Can I turn it in?"* Like they forgot the whole thing, and I'm like WHAAAAT? Middle school students live in the now, so honestly they probably forgot how you felt or looked yesterday, so try to have a fresh start with them instead of rehashing any negative interactions from the previous day.

Once again, my coworker's phrase is ringing, it should go on a plaque. If you want to survive and destress from teaching middle school, I advise you to QUIT TAKING IT PERSONALLY!

Be YOU

The best person you can be is yourself. We tell our students and we tell our own children, but we need to take that advice ourselves. We need to be us to be our best teaching selves.

If I try to be someone I'm not, then I am acting and that is another thing I need to remember to do. It's stressful. For example, I have proudly told you I'm unorganized, so I can't play the organized teacher. Instead, me and the kids laugh about my desk being an explosion zone that eats papers. If I pretended to be organized, I would let students turn in work there and then I would lose it.

I could pretend to be real strict in the classroom where no student talks out of turn and breathes too loud. I'm really more of a chill person and being that uptight would be stressful for me. Some teachers are like that, I'm not so I don't pretend to be. I prefer to make jokes about comments made at inappropriate times or give smiles to students who are expecting me to discipline them.

My mom experienced similar challenges because students were always saying she was so nice. For years she tried to be meaner, stricter, and many other teacher adjectives. She was exhausted from being who she was not. Acting all day as the mean teacher was too much. Finally, she embraced being nice and realized she could build relationships with students and still hold them accountable with consistent and fair expectations. She was herself, and she did better working with students.

It is great for students to get exposed to working with adults who are different from each other and different from them. Hold on to what makes you unique, because you can use it to be a great teacher. Think about the limitations you may have, and how you can use them to be a great teacher. It's okay to admit to students areas where you need help or struggle, because it makes you human. Young teenagers feel very insecure about themselves and it can be a blessing for them to work with an adult who doesn't emulate perfection.

Think About it: Ask yourself these questions to be you in your classroom space.

*How would you describe your personality?
*What strengths do you have that can help you be a great teacher?
*How can you be you and still make it work in your classroom?
*How will you have to adapt the classroom to fit you and your unique strengths and weaknesses?

Keep it Simple

Students are managing a lot on a daily basis. They have seven teachers, 299 other students in their grade, 984 papers in their binder, a demanding social media schedule, 42 passwords to remember, six hours of sleep, four minutes to get to class, and an eight-inch locker to fit all of their crap. All of these stresses are just what we see in building, they also have a life outside the classroom.

Let's do them a favor and KEEP IT SIMPLE. Let's do ourselves a favor and KEEP IT SIMPLE. Some of my colleagues over the years have given me quite a bit of slack for being too easy on the students. I see it differently; I am trying to KEEP IT SIMPLE so they can manage the tasks I have for them.

Here are some ways I keep it simple in my classroom.

Deliver a lesson that will build their background knowledge so they can access assignments. One of the topics I teach is photosynthesis which most students know nothing about. We start talking about plants, when we see them, what do they need to live. If we start talking at this level students can then connect to photosynthesis. I'm not cheating, I'm leveling the playing field for some of my students who have never grown a plant, read a science textbook, or who are learning English as their second language. This idea is more formally known as scaffolding and needs to be built into teaching as a best practice.

Never give out more than one paper for the students to keep per class period. Students get overwhelmed by papers. If they need to read an article and then they are done with it, I make class copies and put them in team folders instead of students having to keep all these papers. It's simple for me because I save time copying, and it's simple for them because they only have what they need in their science section.

Give very clear directions using visual and words. Don't assume they will be able to start with an assignment without clear directions. Try to keep the directions to three steps because you want them to remember all the steps.

Have checkpoints during a class period. Example: You have 10 minutes to read the background section and answer the three review questions. Small checkpoints are going to be more productive than giving students 30 minutes to read the background section, answer the review questions, make a hypothesis, and start writing down the data in the data collection chart. By breaking it down you can check student progress, answer questions and give feedback to help the students throughout the class period instead of finding out at the end of 45 minutes that half of the class did nothing for the whole period.

Don't grade everything. It is okay for students to work on an activity and not collect it or grade it. They are using it as practice or review. You can't grade everything for 150 students every day.

Don't Pretend to know Everything

True Confession: when I first started teaching, I spent hours each night learning everything I could about the topic I was teaching so I could answer any question students may have about the topic. It was tiring to try to stay ahead of my students in that depth of understanding. Why did I feel the need to be so over prepared? Since I was a young teacher, I wanted to be seen as an authority for everything. I wasn't willing to show my human side of not knowing because I didn't want to break this image that I was all knowing. Looking back, I have learned that I can never know the answer to every question a student might ask. As an experienced teacher, I am happy to say I don't know and I didn't even think of that. I'll share ideas that I learn with students in my later classes and give them credit for figuring something out.

It is a free feeling to accept being an imperfect human who doesn't know everything. It can be helpful in building relationships with students when I admit that I don't know everything. I use it to my advantage because now students help me fix all my technology problems with my teacher desktop, Chromebook and projectors. The students feel good about helping me. When students have content questions that I don't know, I use it as a teachable moment where I ask them how we could figure it out. When I have trouble managing something about the class, such as a class having trouble being in our seats at the bell, I ask them what we can do and tell them I can't figure it out without their help. Once you learn its okay to be fallible, it takes a lot of burden off your shoulders and makes it more fun to teach.

Be Consistent

We know that we cannot manage everything all 150 of our students do each day. Choose the expectations that you really stand behind and be consistent every day. I would recommend really only having a few things that you enforce each day. In my classroom, here are some of the priorities that I focus on. I need all students to be on time for learning, listen when I'm talking, not take away the chance for others to learn, and students leave the classroom the way they found it. If students do not follow these expectations, I issue consequences every single time. I start on the first day of school teaching the students what I expect and I repeat it through June. It is draining, but if I'm consistent at the beginning of the year then it will be less of a problem throughout the year. If students know you won't be consistent, they will continue to try things to see what they can get away with in your classroom. If you only follow through sometimes, they feel like they are being targeted and that you are unfair.

We are asked to do too many things as teachers, so we cannot manage everything perfectly. We don't want to be like the waiter, overloaded with plates crashing all around us. Choose what is important to you and enforce it every single time. Even when you have already told students 143 times, go over it again. Even on the day before a break, and with the same student. Every single time.

Think About It: Ask yourself these questions to prioritize things in your classroom.
- What do I need from students each day?
- What cannot happen in my classroom?
- What is important to me as a teacher?
- What things can I let go of?

After you ask these questions, figure out how to tell your students what exactly you need from them. Then, enforce it. Try to let other things slide or you will spend 45 minutes micromanaging every side conversation, cell phone, piece of bubblegum and a million other distractions that slowly make you crazy. If you try to deal with all of those small things like someone having a piece of gum then you are going to start a game of whack a mole where instead of a hammer, you say "don't do that" and then turn around and say "don't do that". This will continue until you wish you had a real whack a mole hammer to use and maybe a strong drink for yourself. 33 kids, 45 minutes, 2 distractions per student. Do the math, it could add up to a lot of wasted energy on small things.

Proximity

The best classroom management is proactive, not reactive. The best classroom management is calm instead of a power struggle. Easy solution: PROXIMITY.

I start on the first day of school making sure that I can access every desk in the classroom and I make loops around my classroom multiple times during a class period. I say that if you are a teacher and you don't get at least 5,000 steps in your teaching time, you aren't moving enough. Since I am always moving around the room, students expect to see me. They know they are being watched. Creepy maybe, effective yes! I use this to help students, to answer questions and to give friendly reminders to stay on task. I visit everyone and make small talk and I visit certain tables multiple times. I am intentional in my walking around the classroom. Most students will do the right thing if they know they are being held accountable, so I use proximity to keep students accountable. Start this at the beginning of the year so students realize that's just how you roll. If proximity is in the daily routine, they don't think you are focusing on them because they are a behavior problem. Besides classroom management, I find it to be a great way to build relationships with individual students. I ask them questions about books they have out, or stickers they have on their binder. I tell them stories about my kids and I ask questions about a club they are in. Students in middle school feel like they get lost and they are not seen by their teachers. Proximity helps to make them feel recognized and important. Students who don't feel comfortable asking questions in a large group will often approach you if you come closer to them.

Proximity is awesome-- just watch out for coffee breath, after lunch onion breath and of course ladies check your shirt/dress to make sure it's safe to lean over a student's desk. If your breath stinks, they will probably tell you and if your shirt is too low cut or shows off your backside they will notice. Plan ahead with mints and a mirror check, and then proximity away.

Even though I don't remember every one of my middle school teachers, I do remember two teachers who really did not have it together. Don't be like them!

Teacher 1: My 7th grade science teacher never left her desk. She would hand out packets (by having a student hand them out) on Monday. She would have a quiz on Friday. She would sit at the front lab table and stare at the class as they worked. She never used any proximity and we never really learned anything or did what we were supposed to do. Don't be glued to the chair. Interact with the students.

Teacher 2: In 8th grade I had a classroom that was kind of small with individual desks in the typical classroom rows. There was no room to move between desks. My poor teacher tried to use proximity, but she was constantly running into people's desks. Without meaning too she was shoving her oversized bottom in students' personal space daily. Don't be this teacher, spread desks out so you can physically fit through and reach each student.

The Power Struggle

A power struggle is when you try to show that you are in charge by meeting a student's words, volume, and actions. If a student feels embarrassed or threatened that amygdala in their brain will fire, and they will keep amping up their responses. An inexperienced teacher will meet them in order to establish authority or because they are angry. An experienced teacher will realize that a student can't talk back if you stop talking. Say as few words as possible and give the student and yourself a chance to calm down.

An example of a simple situation that could lead to a power struggle:

Teacher: Sit in your seat so we can get started.

Student: *I'm going there now so just chill.*

Teacher: Option 1: Give a little wait time and let them get to their seat.

Option 2: Don't tell me to chill, I'm not going to be talked to that way.

This is like choosing a route in a choose your own adventure book, you can probably write the continuation for each response. If you choose option 1 and give them a minute to get to their seat, you can fast forward three minutes and the class is now learning and you can calmly and privately tell the student that you don't appreciate the tone they gave you when you made a simple request. You can ask them how we could do that differently next time.

If you choose option 2, fast forward three minutes and you are upset and you have sunk to the level of the student. They get sent out of class, but really you were equally involved. They get a consequence, you don't. It does seem like in this case the student has a right to play the unfair card. Tomorrow that student knows they can get you upset, so they will try again. The class misses out on a total of 8-10 minutes of instruction watching you engage with a challenging student. The room has lost its calm vibe.

Power struggles show other students that you do not have control over your emotions which can be scary to some students. Power struggles damage your relationship with the student in question, making it so they are more likely to try to get you upset on other days.

Let it Go

Maybe Elsa was right, we really just need to let it go! Stuff happens. You will have kids that you get into it with, you will email parents, you will have kids in for lunch detention. If you have an issue with a student and they have served their appropriate consequence, then you have to let it go! Give the students a new fresh start each day to the best of your ability. Middle school students are usually living in the moment and they have had millions of thoughts since they entered your class yesterday and caused a scene. If you greet them as friendly and approachable, even if you are faking it then you will have more success with the student. Don't let students know that you are still angry or they will move into that threatened lash out phase.

Timers and other cues

If you expect to get the attention of 30 middle school students without any sort of system, either visual or auditory, then good luck. You will be well into retirement age by the time you magically get 30 students to listen without any sort of round up. In order to get the classes attention, you need to have a system and teach them the system.

In my classroom, I love the timer on my computer. It projects through my smartboard speakers. I set it for warmups and during periodic checks during class time. When the timer goes off, voices go off. I say that phrase daily during September until it becomes part of the students training in my class. Remember when you took that psychology class and you learned about Pavlov's dog? He connected the bell with food and then after his training, every time he heard a bell he would drool expecting food. Kids need to be trained. I train them to connect the timer sound with being quiet. The timer end going off is great to get students quiet but the actual timer is great for helping students pace themselves. Many students freak out with a blank assignment, so giving them a set timer for a few questions makes them feel like they can handle the task. If you set a timer, students more likely to get started without wasting time.

Okay so big idea, timers with sound are great. But sometimes I realize my directions were not clear enough or I have too many students off task at one time. How can I get the attention of the class once students are working? You need another signal/system in your room. If I need to get their attention to share some sort of helpful hint or clarify directions, I turn off the lights. When I turn off the lights I say, "Lights off, voices off". I teach them that the lights off is like a time out call on a sports field. I teach them the system and then I make the system work. I don't get 100% of students to respond to timers or lights off, but I will get 75% of the student's attention and then I wait for the others to settle before I give the next directions. I wait for students to comply with the system because as I previously stated, I really don't talk over students. It is not an effective practice.

Some middle school teachers worry about their systems and classrooms feeling too babyish, like they feel like they are in elementary school. I say, let's learn from the expertise of the elementary school teachers. They are amazing and they have so many systems to handle changing subjects, walking quietly through the halls, managing learning centers. If what they do works, let's use it.

- Systems to get students attention:
- Timers
- Some sort of noise maker
- Whistles (not too loud)
- Clapping patterns
- A phrase you say and the students say the second line (call and response)
- Flipping lights on and off

Be creative, be you and find a system that works. Give students signals and directives so they can listen when they need to so they can be successful on assignments.

Be Flexible

I'm giving you pages and pages of advice for being successful at teaching middle school, but I'm telling you all the advice is useless unless you can be flexible. Flexible means that you can expect and accept change. In a perfectly executed science investigation, the scientist will change only one variable to compare results. In a teaching space, the numbers of variables are in the hundreds. There are so many things that you cannot control.

You can't control
- What time buses arrive
- What students are absent
- What kind of mood students are in when they arrive
- Whether or not the wifi is working
- A fire drill in the middle of a quiz
- Changing schedules to accommodate state testing
- Having an assembly during one of your classes
- Breaking of science equipment during a lab

You can control
- How you talk to students
- How you get students who come in late on task
- The mood you are in when you teach
- How you handle technology challenges
- How you plan for longer or shorter classes
- How you catch students up who missed class for an assembly

Notice that all of the things you can control are focused on you. You can only control your own choices. Students are once again looking for us to be calm. If we lose our cool over being interrupted from the office or having eight students at chorus practice, it can be unsettling for kids. In the bigger picture these small interruptions aren't that big of a deal. Skip the review game, spend a little extra time tomorrow, it really doesn't matter. If you are flexible and you can think on your feet, you can make it as a middle school teacher.

Technology

Technology was basically attached to the hands of our students as they entered the world. They knew how to take pictures on a phone at age three. They never experienced a car phone or a beeper. They live in a different world. Technology has been a big push in my district since I started teaching. We have projectors, document cameras, Chromebooks and smart boards. Technology certainly has its place in school. It can be used for virtual field trips, to simulate things in science that we wouldn't be able to see, and certainly in English to type essays. Technology has its place, but it cannot replace teachers.

Technology cannot replace teacher's teaching. Posting an assignment without delivering clear directions does not count as instruction. Students will be logged on doing one of two things with this teaching model.

1. Kids will attempt the assignment and have a million questions.

2. Students will use the technology to play games or do what they want to do. Technology is a tool not a replacement for good teaching.

Technology does not replace real life interactions in the classroom. Most students benefit from hands-on learning. They need to look under microscopes, mix chemicals together and observe objects to see if they are alive or not.

Because students are so comfortable with technology, they use its power for freedom. They know more about technology than most teachers, and if you choose to use it in the classroom you have to understand its limitations, and also understand that you are at a disadvantage. They know how to do more than we know how to do. They know how to quickly have split screens with their assignments on one side and the shooting game on the other side. They know how to hack into websites to view videos and images that are definitely not classroom approved. They know how to share documents with one another so it brings cheating and copying to a new level. They know how to copy and paste from the internet so you have a higher chance of plagiarism.

Old School is Cool

The overuse of technology makes using technology all the time ineffective. If students use technology a lot at school and a lot at home, it's not cool anymore. They don't look forward to using technology when it is so overused. I like to keep technology to a minimum and look for more creative ways to instruct. My old school tool belt is full of ideas that I remember from being in school. The tools I prefer to use are movement, white boards, game shows, and learning stations. As a science teacher, I also have a lot of lab investigations that may not be relevant to other subject areas.

Movement-Students need to move. I worry about students being so sedentary. It's not natural. Wherever I can fit it in to learning I get students moving. Maybe we have a question on the board and they have to agree or disagree. They move to the appropriate side of the room and share with other students their side of the argument. If we are introducing a new unit, they may have a set amount of time to go around the room and do a scavenger hunt for new vocabulary words. I have seen a social studies teacher who set up an assembly line for students in the middle of class to learn about the industrial revolution. Another easy way to implement movement is to them stand up or sit down to answer review questions as true and false. If you structure an activity and give clear directions moving around the classroom creates a great chance for students to learn while having fun.

White Boards-When students see whiteboards on the table, it seems as if they have found a long-lost friend. We use white boards to play review games in class. One game is Pictionary with vocabulary words. Another game is just review trivia where students write one-word answers to a question I provide them. Many math teachers and foreign language teachers use them to review equations and vocabulary. If you do find some of these in a storage closet, I would recommend collecting the markers in between use. Students love to draw on themselves with expo markers and also use up all of the ink with their whiteboard graffiti and drawings. You want it to be a learning tool not a distraction, so use them but plan accordingly.

Jeopardy/Game Show style Games- You can find board game templates for Jeopardy, Hollywood Squares and other games online. Students love to play these and keep track of their points. This can form a nice teamwork atmosphere where students work together for a common goal. This takes a while to set up but if you save it, you have a great resource to use in future years.

Learning Stations-Stations are just small activities that I set up around the room. Each station has a number and a small specific task that needs to be done in a short time. For example, when my students learn about fossils, they have nine stations and a capture sheet. At each station they have to write down notes about a type of fossil, how fossils are formed, or decide whether or not something is a fossil. I could do this as a whole group note taking lesson, but that would be boring. Stations get students moving, working with a small group and gives them a chance to be in charge of their learning. If they have to find the information, they will learn it more in depth. Just remember if you choose to do stations you need clear directions and some sort of timer to keep kids on task. I always make two copies of every station so that four people are not pushing and shoving over one piece of paper. I also put the station resources in plastic sleeves so they do not get destroyed as they are manhandled by 150 students in a day.

When you are planning, make sure you ask yourself how you can engage students with the topic. Think about activities that you remember as a student to see if they spark any creative strategies. Don't be afraid to go old school, old school is cool.

Celebrating Students in non-traditional ways

Middle school students want attention. They are floating around in this growing up purgatory where they don't want to be friends with their teacher, but they want to be recognized and noticed. They need help and guidance, but they want to feel independent. I think knowing this about students makes student celebrations a big deal. All middle school students may not want to be recognized in the same way. At the beginning of the year when I gather basic info on students, I always include a line that says how would you like to be recognized for doing a great job with both public and more private options for celebration. I use these as ways to recognize them through the year. Small recognition like a single piece candy on their birthday or their name on the birthday wall can get kids so excited.

My team has worked really hard to build up positive behavior interventions so we try to amp up the students by recognizing their positive achievements.

Whole Grade Quarterly Celebrations:
Every quarter at lunch we come in one day and present the following paper certificates to students.

Straight A Awards-It's not original but Straight A's are still a big deal worth celebrating.

On a Roll-Students who have made the biggest increase in their GPA. This is my favorite award because the students are always surprised and it ends up being students who usually don't get recognized. It shows that we really want to see progress not perfection in Middle School. This award usually lights a spark under students to keep them motivated.

Character Counts-Students who demonstrate a character trait like responsibility, fairness, helpfulness or whatever the school focuses on. Each teacher and team member picks a secret student and gives them that award. The students are always surprised to see who receives the award and we try to focus on kids who may not be the typical award recipients.

***We celebrate Honor Roll students in a different way. In order to make the celebration seem special and work within a lunch period, we handle Honor Roll at a separate time. Since we keep the awards low in number it is manageable at lunch and also really makes the students feel special about receiving them.

Weekly Team Celebrations:

Weekly Student Notes: At my school we have a weekly team meeting. During those meetings one staff member passes out these forms that we call Student WOWS. Staff members write it like a short letter and include one specific compliment for a student. We keep a log in google docs and try as a team to give every student one before the end of the semester or year. We have student messengers or teachers that deliver them to the students on Fridays during 1st period. Students love these and often slip them in the front of their binders. It is a great and quick way to build relationships, and for us to model positivity to students. We also have similar forms that are Staff to Staff and Student to Staff Wows. All of these positive notes do a great job of increasing morale.

Chapter 5: Saving your own Sanity

Teaching is like housework; it is never finished. If you just reread that for a minute you might see a lightbulb turn on. Keeping this in mind, how do we move forward with the daily challenges that we face that we won't finish? Just like provisioning is a huge part of classroom management, we need to do our own planning to keep our sanity. We need to put ourselves in good headspace to be ready to deal with the students each day. We need to take care of ourselves and we need to help take care of the staff around us.

The Desk clutter problem

In the age of digital it seems that I am more overwhelmed with papers every year. The difference is now I also have digital copies of each of the papers on my desk, which makes my head feel like it is going to explode. I bring all of the clutter I accumulate at school to my desk. I am not proud, but I say this because I want you to know you are not the only one who struggles.

Decluttering my desk because I am so disorganized has had to be a very intentional practice. Here is what I have tried.

- Students are never allowed to put papers on my desk.
- I keep a small recycling bin and trash can next to my desk so I can easily throw away papers like passes and other things I know I don't need right away.
- Every time I go to a meeting and I get papers I don't need; I fold them in half. Later if I find a folded paper, I never relook at it, it goes straight to recycling.
- I put three papers away every day before I leave.
- On my weekly to do lists, I put cleaning my desk on my list every Friday. I never leave on Fridays without a clean desk. This makes me feel like I am ready for a fresh start when I come in on Monday. Let's face it, whatever papers are on my desk aren't going to be relevant on Monday most likely so I might as well get rid of them.
- I keep a 3-hole punch near my desk.
- I keep a three-ring binder in my desk drawer that has tabs for staff meetings, team information, student information, IEPS, 504s, ESOL plans and department. I use this as a safe place to keep papers I probably do need. I pull that out every Friday and file as I clean my desk.
- I have a filing system behind my desk for instructional files. I know we are in the world of digital, but I still need to keep copies or card sorts and stations for students

Since it is close to my desk, I can roll myself over there and put those kinds of activities where they belong. This reduces my stress because it cleans my desk, and I also know it will be there when I need to use it for another lesson.

My desk is not my highlight of my professional accomplishments, but I feel like I have made significant progress. Be intentional about it, and attack it in small manageable segments, and you will see the same success.

Never leave school without being ready for the next day

Teaching is so tiring. You are exhausted at the end of the day you have nothing left. All you want to do is to leave to the safety of your car and possibly make a late afternoon Starbucks run. As tempting as it may be to leave at the end of the day, don't leave without being ready for the next day. And by being ready, I mean you have the slides to share with students, the activity copied, and all of the manipulatives or student materials that you need. You have highlighters or colored pencils ready to hand out to students. Even if this takes an extra ten or fifteen minutes, it is so worth it.

Why do you need to be ready? You never know what is going to happen in the morning. You may hit traffic, can't find a matching set of shoes, your dog gets loose or any other number of events that could cause you to be late. If these things happen, which they will, then being prepared means you can still have a productive day of learning with your students. You can be calm and in control. Other teachers are not taking this advice, so even if you arrive on time, don't rely on a working copier in the morning. More than likely there are either four teachers waiting to use the copier or it is already overheating and jammed by the time you can use it. Plan ahead and have copies made for the next day of instruction.

Back to School Night Basics

September is crazy stressful for teachers. Teachers make it through the stress of preservice just in time to get ready for the stress of the first week. In most schools as soon as you have a chance to breathe you see the dreaded email in your inbox: Back to school night next week!

For many teachers Back to School Night is a very stressful event. I wanted to share some insight on how to turn this major stressor into a great opportunity to connect with families.

DO:

- Dress in an outfit that makes you feel confident (I usually bring one to change into so I don't look sweaty and risk spilling coffee on it)
- Brush your teeth and reapply deodorant before the event so you won't be questioning whether you smell or they are enjoying the remnants of the onion soup you had for dinner
- Prepare an electronic PowerPoint or google slides to guide the conversation so you don't have to rely on memory
- Put the first slide with your name and room number so parents can check their schedules to see if they are in the right place
- Meet families at the door to shake hands (this also helps if parents can't navigate the school map)
- Be yourself: If you like sports share a bitmoji with you as a quarterback, like to tell jokes have some cheesy one liners ready, love reading share one of your favorite books- Mention a little bit about yourself inside and outside of school

For example: This year I am really excited about teaching …. And also my first trip to Disney World over Christmas break. They want to see you as a human

- Cover a <u>very basic</u> overview of curriculum and classroom structure. For example: We start each day with activators, students are seated in groups because we really value collaboration, students will use google classroom regularly
- Share how students will be graded and opportunities you provide to support student learning
- Practice going through your slides and time yourself to see if the information you want to present fits in the time you have
- Have a copy of your email address accessible-this will eliminate any potential phone tag drama
- Share upcoming important events in the school
- End your presentation by saying thank you for coming, building the parent teacher relationship is so important for students to be successful

DON'T:

- Wear heels if you have never worn them before-Be comfortable
- Spend too much time going over every little thing the children will learn, the parents are about as interested as the kids who crumbled up your syllabus and left it on the floor
- Tell parents you are a first or beginning teacher-even if you are, even though you know what you are doing it may give parents some ground to question you
- Hold parents after the bell
- Finish with too much time left because it makes you look unprepared and opens up the floor for comments and questions you are too tired to engage in
- Allow parents to start a mini parent teacher conference
- Have only one sign in by the door that limits people being able to get into the classroom space
- Ask open-ended questions like, "Does anyone have any questions?" You are already nervous and tired and may not have the best response to an unpredicted question

- Give out too much personal information or your personal phone number

Sharing a classroom without losing your mind

Middle school classrooms sometimes have to be shared, and it kind of sucks. My classroom has been used for the last three years for a class during one of my periods off. Selfishly I wish I didn't have to share. Of course you feel the same way, but life isn't perfect. Even though you don't want to share, remember it is often harder on the teacher who is coming into your room, so try to be accommodating.

There are several things you can do to make sharing a classroom more manageable. First, talk to the other teacher. Ask them about how they run their class, how they like to present their materials, and what space they would like to use in your classroom for student materials. They may need to store textbooks, folders or something else for student use. By asking them what space they need, you are building a relationship with the other teacher and making them feel welcome in your space. Next, tell them how you run your classroom and procedures you have in place. You need to tell them the expectations for how materials are used in your room so they can hold their students to the same level of responsibility. For example, in my space Chromebooks are never left on tables, and students do not get materials from my bookshelves without teacher permission. Students are not allowed to sit at my desk. These are three things that really bother me so telling the other teacher ahead of time alleviates any stress and frustration from different expectations. Once you set these guidelines, you can check in every week or so to see how things are going for both of you. Remember we are here for students, not for our own petty battles.

Some other small things that you can do to be helpful are to move out when they come in. Give them access to your desk without your half-eaten lunch and plan book spread out. Leave the room if possible so they don't feel like they are being watched. Give them copies of things like blank seating chart grids and fire drill procedures so they don't have to recreate those things for each of the classrooms they travel to. Include the teacher's name and period they use your room on sub plans so subs know they will need to leave your space during that time. Try to keep your desk clean and accessible to them so they can work effectively. Also, if you see them doing something great while you are coming in or leaving tell them. Positive recognition goes a long way to build positive relationships with staff.

How to use your Planning time Effectively

Let's start with the obvious, you cannot get everything done in the limited 45 minutes planning period you have a day in middle school. With that said, you want to use that precious time as effectively as you can. I have provided some dos and don'ts that have worked for me and hopefully will work for you.

DO

*Make lists

      I keep a small spiral notebook on my desk at all times. I create two columns Today and This Week. Throughout the day I add things to both sides of the list. I am very specific when I write things on the list, for example instead of writing grade papers, I list the assessment and class periods that need to be graded. This has two benefits; one I have a plan for when I finally sit down, and two I get the satisfaction at crossing more things one at a time off my list.

*Make yourself inaccessible

      I turn off my lights and close the door so I am not distracted by the learning and excitement of nearby classrooms. This also deters students and staff that want to stop by from finding me. I'm not being selfish, I am being honest, I have too much to do in too little time.

*Make sure you are planned for the next day

      Most districts focus on collaborative long-term planning and backmapping. All of this is great to have a big picture idea for planning. Also, it is super important to make sure you have everything in place for the next day. I do a little checklist to make sure I have everything covered: lesson ideas, copies, slides or presentation, materials. After I cover those categories I spend a few minutes with the nitty gritty. I ask myself these types of questions:

how long will this take, are they working alone or with a partner, how will I summarize the lesson. These questions make the class period run smoother.

DON'T

*Go to the copier empty handed

Sometimes you have to spend valuable time waiting in front of the dreaded copier. In case you have one of those days, plan ahead by bringing a set of papers with you or a plan book to think about what you're going to do next week. This way you can maximize your efficiency.

*Spend 10 minutes chatting with a coworker

We all need time to vent after a rough student interaction or an annoying parent email. Set a time limit if you need to chat and choose someone who is quick and to the point. Get over it, and get back to work. You will be more upset later when you realize how much time you wasted with no solutions.

*Check your email every time you hear a BING

I get at least 20 emails a day. Some days it might be closer to 40. If I want to focus on grading, I sit at a table in my room not at my desk so I am not tempted to check my email every time I hear a new email coming in. Most times it ends up being an email sent to staff and then a variety of responses from staff who don't understand the difference between reply and reply all on an email. None of these situations are urgent enough to take my precious grading time away. It can all be dealt with later.

*Focus on unnecessary things

This year I will teach five classes in a row before going to planning. I am mentally and physically fried during planning. In my state of health I sometimes find myself doing irrelevant tasks during planning. Some examples of irrelevant tasks include throwing out all of the empty glue sticks, cleaning tables with clorox wipes, emptying the pencil sharpener---you get the idea. Many of these tasks can be done in the morning as students are getting settled or even better, they can be done by a student instead.

Share some Love with your team

Teaching can be lonely. The building is filled with 1,000 moving bodies, but you feel alone. Other adults are trapped in their own classrooms and you are stuck with thirty 12-year-olds in your classroom. You can't use the bathroom when you want, and you are so over trying to get all this testing done. See...it can be lonely. One way to feel more connected is to spread some love and positive vibes to other staff. More than likely other teachers feel lonely too. Try to build some relationships with your team so you can all feel connected.

Easy Team Builders for Staff:
- Invite another staff member to eat lunch with you
- Ask another teacher about their day and actually listen to their response
- Ask another teacher about something in their life outside of school
- Leave a little candy in their mailbox
- Bring snacks to a team meeting
- Write a positive note to another staff member who did something great
- Tell them something great you overheard a student say about them
- Post a funny meme in the staff bathroom
- Sit with someone new at a staff meeting
- Let someone go before you at the copy machine

Keep it Positive

Typically, during pre-service week everyone in the building is positive. Every staff member is tan, refreshed and full of optimism. Slowly September drains the positive energy and creativity as teachers get completely overwhelmed. It's not our fault, servicing 800 students from the ages of 11-14 and all of their parents is not for the faint of heart. So, what can we do to maintain a positive climate where we feel less edgy?

I think some of the answers surround staff morale. Although it may seem like that is the job of administration, I think it's everyone's job to keep it positive. I have worked with a wonderful team and in my classroom to build a positive space. I hope these ideas spur your own creative ideas on how to spread the love so to speak.

For the grade level team I work on, we started using part of our team time to write thank you notes. Sometimes, the notes were intended for other staff members. Just a quick two sentence specific note that told them something they did that helped or encouraged us during the week. We mass copied the template and left them in our team office and the main office work room. It felt so good to get one in your mailbox, that it really picked up some steam with more staff members trying it. I keep a stack in my desk drawer and make it a weekly goal to fill one out. Now we have extended it to include student to staff, staff to student. We hope this continues to spread the positive message that is so important for middle school students.

Okay, so maybe old-fashioned note writing isn't your style. How else can you keep it positive? I find that classroom decor goes a long way towards positivity. I fill my classroom with things that make me happy. I have pictures of my family around the room so students can see into my life a bit and for me to have constant reminders that I am blessed. I particularly love Disney movies and print pictures of characters to use for classroom rules or just posters with quotes.

They are colorful and fun and for other students who like Disney, it is an easy way to establish connections at the beginning of the year. I make a mystery teacher investigation on the first day when I ask students to find out about me. This will bring out some great conversation starters that build a positive relationship. On a daily basis, one of the biggest things I do is that I address students by name so they know they matter as an individual. That is so important for students who are in the process of trying to figure out who they are.

Staff can be challenging, because after pre-service week you rarely see all of those individuals that you worked on teambuilding activities with. I try to smile when I see teachers in the hall. Making eye contact and smiling is a free way to be positive. I also tell them things I heard they were doing that the students enjoyed. If nothing else seems to work, you can always bond over your common frustration with the copier. Talk to other teachers and they will usually respond positively. If I find teachers who tend to be in the negative zone, I still pass on the happy smiles but distance myself from engaging in any more conversations. My day is difficult enough without added stress, so it is okay to set boundaries around people who bring you down. Keep it civil without feeling the need to press further in a relationship.

Success for Subs

Eventually you will have to be out of the classroom. You will get sick or have to attend a meeting. You hope that the systems you have in place will be able to keep your classroom walls standing during your absence. With that in mind, you want to set your sub up for success to make the day run as smoothly as possible for the sub, your students and your physical classroom.

How do you help a sub without spending hours preparing?

1. At the beginning of the year, I write a general sub plans page with all essential information.

- Teaching schedule with times, classes, and lunch
- Other classes that may meet in your classroom
- General classroom directions on how your students work in your space
- Fire Drill/Emergency Procedures
- Student helpers for each class
- Teachers/room numbers to go to if they need help.
- A note to leave names of students who were helpful during the class period
- A big thank you-subs who take middle school jobs are angels in the flesh

2. A current list of attendance and seating charts for each class period in an easily accessible location.

3. When planning, plan for things that model your normal instruction. For example, if you always start with an activator, then leave an activator for the sub also.

4. Create easy to manage activities with only one paper per student. Plan an activity that students can do on their own because the sub may or may not have the content knowledge. Some examples

that may work: review activities, previewing new content with a textbook, crossword or other vocabulary-based puzzles. I have found that pre-printed worksheets are easier for students than blank paper and questions from the book.

5. Plan more than you think they will get done. If students are busy then there is less room for discipline issues. Always make sure to have subs tell students that the work will be collected and graded because they need to be held accountable for their work.

You already know students who will be a problem when you are not in class, because most times they are the same students who are problems when you are in class. Encouraging positive notes about students is helpful when you return. I make a big deal about the positive student list. I give out a small candy, little school bucks or erasers as a thank you. I hope it will help more students behave the next time I need to be out.

The inevitable parent Email

Most middle school students will do what you want them to do with simple guidance and structure. Other students need more individual interventions, and one of the common interventions is a parent contact, which is usually in the form of an email. Don't be afraid to write an email to parents, but be smart when you email parents.

DO

- Remember that we live in a digital world where anything you write is going to be out there. Emails can be shared and reshared once they are sent. Deleting emails does not make them go away.
- Remember this is someone's child, so they love this child and they are going to want to be on the child's side
- Be specific about your concern without being judgmental
- Include positive things about the child
- Re-read your email twice before sending it
- Include your name and the subject you teach in the email
- Include the connection to student learning. Some parents might not be worried if their child is out of their seat all the time, but they are more likely to care if you mention that you are concerned that the student is not able to access their learning material because they are out of their seat many times during class.
- Use classroom management strategies before emailing. Have you talked to the student, moved their seat, handled the same situation more than twice? If you have, it may be time to send an email.
- Follow up if you see positive changes in the area of concern

DON'T

- Give your opinions on why a child did something
EXAMPLE: Jon was disrupting class again and he didn't care that the class was supposed to be working.
- Write an email when you are very upset. Leave yourself a note to do it later once you are calm so you don't put too much emotion into the email.
- Expect a response
- I find that most times parents read emails. You may not have left a question, or maybe they didn't know how to respond. Don't assume that it was unread.
- Tell parents how something should be handled. Every family has different systems in place and they have their own strategies for discipline. If you suggest what they should do, you are really overstepping your professional boundaries.

Sometimes if you have a very specific behavior concern, it may be easier to contact the parent by phone. Phones can be a solution for typing out a whole long conversation.

Since I teach so many students, sometimes I find myself typing the same email over and over again. This year I got smarter, and I typed a document called generic emails. I use them and edit in their names as needed. I spent time crafting these emails so I don't have to reread them and make sure the words address my concern for the student without being accusatory. I wrote email templates for the four most common emails I send.

Email Shell
Here are some samples of generic emails that I use in my classroom. After I send these to parents, I put a copy in the school communication log. (These are included in the free resource using my online link.)

Grades
My name is _____ and I am your child's (subject) teacher. I am writing to let you know that I am currently concerned about your child's grade in my class. I know that your student is very capable of earning a C or better in my class, but their current grade is not reflecting their ability. Here are some things that I can do to help your child. Students are able to retake quizzes they are not successfu

on during class time. They can retake two quizzes per quarter if they talk to me. They can also ask for help at lunch. You can help your child by checking their grades weekly online and encouraging them to redo assignments they struggled with. Thank you for supporting your student in their learning.

(You can always add specific assignments and suggestions to the shell, but it gives you a place to start.)

Cell Phones

Cell phones are the downfall of secondary teaching today. Hopefully your school and district have developed plans for managing cell phones. More than likely, you are like me. My school and district have a plan but cell phones are still an issue.

My name is _____ and I am your child's (subject) teacher. I wanted to let you know that the school district rule for cell phones is _____. I am concerned that your child is not following these guidelines in the classroom. I have noticed that the cell phone is becoming a daily distraction for your student. I give three reminders a class period and your student is still using their phone. When students are on their phones, they are missing instruction. They are also distracting other students from learning because they are involving them with their phones. I want all of my students to be able to access their learning, and I wanted to let you know that currently your students cell phone is limiting their access to their academics. Thank you for your support in your students' learning.

Behavior

My name is _____and I am your child's (subject) teacher. I wanted to let you know that I am concerned about some of your child's choices in the classroom. I know how capable your student is, and recently I have seen a change in their behavior. Some of the things I am seeing in class include (limit to 2 or 3 behaviors). To help your student make better choices I have _____. I am concerned that these choices are taking away from your child's academic success as well as the academic success of their peers in the classroom. I would really appreciate it if you could talk to your child about how capable they are, and how we both want them to be successful in class. Thank you for your support.

(I try to write emails to parents when I start to see some negative changes, so that we can prevent higher level infractions. I can document that I have involved the parents. This kind of early intervention can help build a relationship with parents if you ever need to involve them later on. Also, if I see that the student is turning it around, I like to send a positive follow up email a week or so later.)

Not Prepared for Class

My name is _____ and I am your child's (subject) teacher. I am writing to let you know that your child is continually coming to class without their proper materials. Students are expected to come to class with their binder, papers and a writing utensil. Having all three of these materials will ensure that your student is coming to class ready to learn. Your student is coming to class without _____ each day. If they need to borrow materials from me they miss the first few minutes of instruction. I don't want your student to get behind so I would like them to come to class prepared. If you are able to help your students get some _____ to use for class it would benefit their learning. Thanks in advance for your support. If you are in need of assistance in supplying school supplies please contact me.

25 dollars that Saved my Sanity

Teacher supplies are fun to buy, but prices can really add up. Before you start spending a whole paycheck, make sure you buy the essentials that you will use regularly. I have listed my classroom organization systems that I have purchased for under $25.00

5 different colored plastic folders
I spent $1.25 on each of the five folders seven years ago, and I use the folders each day. I use one color for each of my five sections. Inside the colored folder, I label the left-hand side with GRADED and the right-hand side with UNGRADED. All the work goes from the turn in bins to the folder so I never have the chance to lose it in the massively growing pile of papers on my desk.

12 pack of medium binder clips
When you have a whole class set of papers, paper clips can easily detach and have papers flying across the room. I prefer to clip each set of papers with a medium binder clip. Papers will stay together even if the folder falls on the floor or anything else happens. They can be reused for each new set of papers that will be waiting for you when you finish grading the current set.

4-3 drawer plastic bins that hold 8.5 x 11 paper
I have a sign on my desk that says Papers enter at your own risk as a fun way to remind them that there is a proper place to turn in work. I use two sets of 8.5 X 11 bins (3 drawers each) for turn in bins for each class I teach. I label each drawer with a color to match the colors for the class folder. This system makes it easy for students to be able to turn in their own work without any help from me. I use the other 2 sets of drawers and label it with the days of the week. I put all resources for the next week in my drawers before I leave on Friday and that makes me leave feeling calm and as prepared as I can be for Monday morning.

If you have any money left, I like to splurge on Papermate Flair Pens.These inexpensive pens last all year and come in bright colors so they don't blend in with any colors the students write with. They are markers so they feel fun to write with. In addition to grading they work great for colorful doodling during staff meetings if necessary.

The years of teaching

As with most people who went into education, I wanted to make a difference with students. Maybe you had a parent like I did that was an educator or you were inspired by a positive teaching role model in your life. If you are like me the way you pictured your teaching career and the way it ended up don't always line up.

I remember talking to a veteran teacher friend my 3rd or 4th year of teaching. I would compare myself to her and constantly feel frustrated. How did she keep up with all of her grading and parent contacts and make it look so easy? Every day seemed like a struggle to me. She told me of course I was struggling, to wait until my tenth year and then I would be a master teacher. I held that advice close to my heart and I started to see each year that something had gotten more manageable. Just like with students if you want to see progress as a professional you can't just look day to day, you have to look at larger blocks of time. Don't be hard on yourself if you are not mastering everything. Instead, think positive and focus on all of the new things you have learned. Give yourself an air high five for learning how to plan daily and weekly lessons, use classroom technology, work with an online gradebook, and how to built lasting relationships with students.

If you are starting a new year, put those optimistic lenses on and reflect. What went well last year, what will you do differently this year. Give yourself credit for where you were successful and give yourself a manageable goal to work towards in an area that needs improvement. Set one or two goals at the most. I write notes to myself about my goals and post them on my plan book where I will see them often to reference back to.

Here are some examples of goals that I have made for myself over the last several years.
*Put out all of the papers in an organized way for the next week
*Plan lessons at least a week out

*Send more positive notes to students
*Add in at least one fun brain break activity for the week
*Update gradebook twice a week

Teacher Stress

You can't cruise social media without finding memes indicating that teaching is a stressful job. While we teachers laugh at them, we laugh because they are true and we feel it every day. That is the same reason we feel like ringing the necks of the next person who tells us that it must be nice to work 10 months a year. I always reply to people that I have managed enough stress and graded enough assignments for a comparable 12-month year job.

Since teacher stress is a real thing, how do teachers deal with it? I can't speak for all teachers so I suggest asking around and seeing what people suggest to manage the stress but I can share what I have tried.

One thing that keeps me grounded is to realize that a teacher's work is never going to be finished. While it sounds like a real downer, its reality so I don't constantly seek to attain the unattainable. Second, I think about things I can control and things I can't. If a situation falls under out of my control, I do my best to mentally leave it at work. Third, I look for stress triggers and try to deal with them in an appropriate way. The last and most difficult stress reliever for me is to leave it at work. While it may seem impossible, it can be done at least to some extent with some proactive steps.

Step 1: I can't get everything done.
I keep a running to do list on my desk at all times. I keep adding two things every time I take off one. I always pick three items that I will finish before leaving school that day. I make my list very specific making it measurable and attainable. For example, if I have quizzes to grade, I will list the periods to be graded because I can't ever finish grading five sets of papers in any sitting. I leave everyday feeling accomplished because of those scribbled out notes. If I get more than three items crossed off then I walk out of school feeling like a Rockstar.

Step 2: Can I control it?

Sort the stressors into two categories and then deal with them appropriately. I vent about the out of my control and get it out of my system. Once I have properly vented which may be required more than once depending on the situation, I have to move forward. I reflect on the in my control box and make changes.

In My Control: Be honest about your concerns and then REFLECT on how to fix it.

- The class did not do well on an assessment.
  Reflect: Maybe I can make a review game or group work and allow for an in-class retake.

- I lost my cool with a student.
  Reflect: What will the conversation be between me and the student   tomorrow.

- I do not have lesson plans for next week.
  Reflect: What do the students need to know? What resources do I have   that I can use?

- Every day I am coming home with a headache.
  Reflect: Am I drinking enough water and getting enough sleep? Do I need to meditate or maybe a quick mini-kickboxing session at lunch? Maybe I need to schedule a run or a walk with a friend before or after work.

Out of my Control: Process that it is frustrating, and then move on.

- My school requires a minimum of 10 quizzes in a grading period.
- My principal has observed me already and is back in my room in less than a month
- My co-teacher is not someone I like working with
- I had to cover classes when we had five people out without subs

- I sat in traffic for an extra 20 minutes because of an accident
- The parent I emailed never emailed me back
- I got two new students added to my class in the last week

Step 3: Identify the stress triggers and deal

These are a few of the stress triggers that I have dealt with personally. You may have your own list or maybe you share some of my stressors.

#1 Long Commute

Ways to Deal:
- Short term-try different routes and times of leaving in the morning
- Enjoy the opportunity to listen to your favorite music or podcast. Make it time you enjoy for yourself.
- Long-term-Look into schools closer to home (I am a spoiled brat with a 5 minute commute and I have to say I am sooooooo much happier. I have an extra hour of my life each day)

#2 Students are not Listening to Directions

Ways to Deal:
- Don't talk till they are quiet
- Be clear with expectations
- **Prepare slides with visuals to keep students engaged in directions**
- Take deep breaths
- Let them try it without you and watch them squirm and suffer until they realize your instructions are vital to their very being

#3 So many emails

Ways to Deal:

- If it doesn't apply to me then delete it without reading
- If it does apply to me read it and delete as soon as possible
- Example: The email says you need to fill out a form for Jared by this date.
    Fill out form
    Email form
    Delete email and do a celebration dance at your desk
    Cross it off your to do list with a bright colored pen and do one more small celebratory dance

Step 4: Leave it at work

Leaving work at work sounds impossible for teachers, but you need to treat teaching like any other career where it stays at work. There is a time to work and a time to play. For the first few years you may need to do some planning or grading at home, but don't develop this as a regular habit. Working all the time leads to burnout. I leave my grading at school. I know this is not typical for most people, but for me it keeps me sane. The last time I brought a big stack of quizzes home my 7-year-old daughter wanted to help. In her process of helping she wrote on them with a thick marker, spilled her water bottle on most of them and dropped my organized pile onto the floor. The time it took me to recover the papers was time I used to remind myself to leave papers at work. On the rare occasion I do take papers home, I only take things home if I have a plan for them and if I set limits. For example, I may say I will grade these multiple-choice quizzes while my son is at practice, and then I am not doing anymore. I laugh when kids ask me the day after a quiz if I have graded them yet, because I haven't. I then ask them if they spent two hours of their own time reading up and studying science the night before. They look at me with this weird expression until they get what I mean. We all staff/students have a life outside of school and results are not always immediate. Sometimes you have to wait. This idea is a challenge for middle schoolers today who are so used to immediate results. Another helpful leave it at work strategy has to do with email. In the age of technology, we are always connected, but that doesn't mean we have to stay connected to work. I avoid any email checking while I'm at home. Can you think of any times when you were happy about something you read in a work email at home? Yeah me neither, so I stopped doing it. I find it easier to manage all of the things at school when I give myself a break from it. It becomes part of self-preservation that gets me through the year without having to use coffee injections.

Chapter 6: Final Thoughts and Words of Wisdom

You are Doing Enough

Teaching is a draining profession. It seems to be an unwritten rule that teachers are always inspired, giving, creative, understanding, but also firm and consistent. Teachers feel bad about taking off, because we are so needed in the classroom. After you feel like you have given more than you have to offer, you see a list of new expectations.

The school system is compiled of a hierarchy of demands. New initiatives and expectations trickle down to us classroom teachers in a way where it is easy to feel defeated.

We know that we obviously have to plan lessons, teach lessons, and grade lessons. However, there are so many additional things that we also need to do.

Here are some examples:
- Build positive relationships with every student in your class
- Give timely feedback on all assessments to help student learning
- Integrate culture and math into lessons
- Differentiate your instruction to reach all readiness levels in your space
- Contact all parents who have students whose scores have gone down or who have Ds and Es in your class
- Cover classes for teachers who do not have subs
- Describe and collect data on a set of focus students and how you are going to measure their progress this year
- Be emotionally available for students who may need emotional support
- Fill out forms to update all of the student IEPs
- Collect anecdotal data on how many times a certain student exhibits a certain behavior

- Stand in the hallways during each transition to welcome students into the classroom
- Set up community circles for students to have a voice in your classroom
- Catch students up who was absent for three weeks traveling out of the country
- Help students the last week of the quarter bring up their grade from the entire quarter
- Bring students reading level up from the 3-grade level deficit
- Be more engaging than what is on their phones

Just writing this list makes me feel stretched thin, and a little bit angry. I know that all of these ideas are great suggestions for the classroom. We live in a time where there are obvious learning gaps and students are coming to school with more and more emotional needs. As teachers we sometimes are the most consistent adult in the lives of these students. However, we are still human. Just remember you are doing enough. You come to work each day planned for instruction. With the help of coffee and patience, you hold your head up and try your best each day. You never know what you are walking into with 150 middle school students, so you do the best you can.

I take all of these initiatives as a guiding principle. I use them as something to strive for, with the understanding that my sacred 45 minutes a day will not be able to cover all of these ideas. I try to choose one specific goal for the year that I really focus on. Start with small changes that you can make such as call students by name, or include a summarizer each day. Once I master that goal, I can incorporate what I have learned and take on a new goal. That is how you slowly over time become a master teacher. As for all of the school system demands, I stay open-minded about what they are sharing without drowning myself with stress and pressure over implementing them.

It's so easy to be pressured to give more than you have to offer. I used to give too much, and then I realized it was taking away my own personal happiness. I had no mental and emotional energy for my family at home or to take care of myself. Just like flight attendants tell you to put on your oxygen mask before helping someone else, take care of yourself, and then give what you can to others. Teaching is hard, and you are doing enough!!

Start Each Day with a Fresh Start

Do you like to drink yesterday's coffee? You know the one that's been sitting in the coffee maker at room temperature with all of the coffee grounds settled to the bottom. Of course no one wants to drink yesterday's coffee. You want to move forward and have a fresh start to your day. Your new coffee is going to smell amazing; it's going to be hot and energize you for the day ahead. Just like the fresh coffee, we need to start each day with a fresh start in our classrooms. If yesterday didn't go well, make adjustments for today. There are no positive results that come from dwelling over what happened yesterday without making a plan to move forward. There are going to be lots of days that don't go as planned. Learn from them and reset.

Here are some of the ways to start fresh each day.

1. **Forgive Yourself**-Teachers put too much pressure on themselves to have everything run smoothly. There are times when the lesson will be boring, messy, unorganized, and many other adjectives. You are not a bad teacher if a lesson doesn't go well. All teachers become better teachers from learning from these teachable moments.

2. **Forgive Students**-Students in middle school say and do foolish things as part of their brain construction. Don't target students and say things like, "Today needs to be better than yesterday," or give them the angry eyes over an event that happened yesterday. Instead, greet each student with a friendly greeting. Remember, they have forgotten yesterday, so you should do the same.

3. **Apologize and fix problems**-It's okay to admit to students that you are sorry for getting frustrated or that you apologize for running out of time. It's also okay to tell them that you are going to give more clear directions so that no ones, or that you will give them extra time to finish since they were rushed. Students respond well

when you acknowledge how you made them feel, or are sorry about something that happens. You are human, and it's okay for them to see that.

4. **Try Something New**- If you feel like you are losing student engagement or if you are struggling to manage class behaviors, try something new. You can try new seating charts, new ways of grouping students, new teaching style, or new instructions.

5. **Restate Expectations**- Don't assume that going over the expectations during the first week of school is enough to guarantee good choices for the whole school year. Students needs refreshers on expectations throughout the year once they get a little too comfortable or when you start to see an increase in class disruptions. Experienced teachers build in time to review expectations as needed so students remember what you expect and get a fresh start to meet your expectations.

6. **Start Where you Left Off**- Don't move on to another topic until you have reached closure on one topic or assignment. You may do a quick review game or give a few extra minutes to finish something from the day before. When you leave students to finish assignments on their own you often have missing assignments, and struggling students often have difficulty without your proper assistance.

Lessons from an Injury

This past December I encountered some very surprising blessings after spending over a month with a broken hand. I broke my dominant left hand when I made a mistake trying to break a board in a Tae Kwon Do belt test. It didn't hurt as bad as you might think. I went to work the next day and then my husband convinced me to go to urgent care after my hand was blue. The throbbing pain and the Christmas color cast doesn't sound like a blessing does it? In my time of slowing down with my injury, I learned some valuable lessons and I am blessed because of it.

Lesson 1: Rest

This year I teach five classes in a row. I can barely use the bathroom, and by the time I get to my planning period I am exhausted both physically and mentally. During the morning classes I usually jot down 20 things on my to-do list, and then frantically start working on the list as soon as the last group of students exits the door. Once I hurt my hand I couldn't easily add to the list, so I was feeling less frantic at the start of planning. For the first two weeks after my injury I really needed to physically rest so I found myself taking a short stroll to clear my head, or sitting and reading something funny or inspirational from a blog while I held my hand above my heart to increase circulation. After I felt the throbbing go down, I would do my normal planning routine. Once I had taken time to rest, I was ready to take on the next challenge.

At home, like all teachers my house is its own chaotic circus. The kids, the dogs, the dishes and the laundry all seem to call to me and sometimes they seem suffocating. During the first two weeks I told myself and the inanimate objects in my house that I was on a break. I wasn't up to inside outing each sock in the laundry or scraping peanut butter off breakfast plates. When I heard myself telling off the laundry, it felt good. I just rested and it was good. I told the kids I couldn't sit and play board games and toy figures with them. They came up with alternative ideas. My daughter read books to me and my son sat with me while we watched a non-cartoon movie. Both kids worked together to help me make dinner and clear and set the table. I rested and it was good. I went to bed at 9:00 and it was good.

Lesson 2: Ask for help

I truly never appreciated the things that my left hand does each day, until I didn't have it to use. Simple procedures like using a zipper and putting on socks work so much better with two hands. Watching my 7-year-old cheer me on as I attempted putting on my socks was both humbling and entertaining. I realized that it was okay to ask for help. Once I got up the nerve to ask for help, people were more than happy to lend a hand. (Pun intended.) My family made sure to check that I was dressed and my work bag zippered before they got ready to leave. My mom and daughter helped me grade the papers I brought home.

At school I also had to ask for help. Students passed out activities. They collected and sorted materials we finished with so I could put them back in my files. I used one of my hyperactive students to hand out the PBIS bucks to students who answered review questions and stayed on task. I found that asking for help gave me a chance to build new relationships. Many students benefited from having responsibilities in the classroom. I also reminded myself that students should be organizing materials when they leave every day because they can be responsible and it saves me so much time. Other neighboring teachers helped me assemble labs each day and even helped me zip my coat before leaving. This gave me a chance to have some little conversations with other teachers. It reminded me that even though teaching can make you feel isolated we are all better off if we have positive relationships with adults in the building. Other teachers get your struggles, and they too are probably looking for some positive adult interactions. Asking for help at home and school ended up being a win-win for me.

Lesson 3: Prioritize

One of the most exhausting things for me as a teacher is the never finishing. The papers, emails and forms pile up quicker than I can finish them. With my hand out of commission, it made me prioritize what I was going to work on each day. Some ways I handled my physical limitations was to warn the students that I wasn't going to be able to provide written feedback on everything, I also decided not to grade some of the labs I collected. I sat in meetings and just listened since I couldn't write any notes. I focused on one day of instruction at a time making sure I had everything ready for just the next day instead of the whole next week. I even took time off work to go to the doctors twice in one month because my physical well-being was more important than any of the papers or things waiting for me at work.

If you have ever taught in December you know it brings out the worst in both students and teachers. New and experienced teachers alike survive on caffeine and sugar. Usually teachers need four to five days of winter break to become human again. This year was one of the best Decembers I have ever had since becoming a teacher. It may be that the Christmas colored cast was a constant reminder of the joy of the season, but I really think it was the time that I took to rest, ask for help, and prioritize. After this experience I was ready to move forward in January after readjusting how I operated at both home and school.

If you are injured, stressed, or completely exhausted try some of these tips to make it through the day a little easier:

Rest:

- If you're sick, stay home. Resting will prevent you from getting a more serious illness that requires you to miss more time.
- Physically sit down for a few minutes during class and on your planning.
- Take deep breaths anytime you feel yourself getting frustrated or overwhelmed.
- Read a book at home for fun.
- Take a short walk during the school day. Invite a colleague and enjoy a little walk and talk if you want to both exercise and vent.
- Pick at least 1-2 days a week to leave work at work. Don't grade papers at home or check emails.

Ask for help:
- Delegate tasks in the classroom to students (Examples include: checking homework, handing out assignments, fixing something on the Chromebook)
- If you are having trouble with a student, ask other teachers on your team what they have tried
- Be bold and speak up in the areas you need support. Other trusted teachers, administrators and counselors can only help you if they know you need help.

Prioritize:
- Delete emails (without reading them) that have nothing to do with you
- Decide what has to be done today and start there
- Take your time replying to emails, you have at least a 24-hour grace period

Don't feel bad adjusting your expectations for yourself if you are injured or if you have a lot of stress. All you can do is give 100% of what you are capable of each day. In sickness and in health, these three simple ideas can make teaching more manageable. Don't feel guilty resting, asking for help and prioritizing!

Middle of the road teacher

When I read online articles about teaching, I always feel a bit nauseous and exhausted. Why you may say, it's because I never see myself in the posts I read. It seems 60% of the education blogs and posts are from teachers who hate their job. They want to show that they are a martyr by taking a job in education. They sacrifice their personal time, sanity and planning time to make sure everything is perfect for their classroom. These posts and articles point out all my daily frustrations and then make me suddenly aware of three to four new frustrations I was previously unaware of. These blogs make me exhausted, and truthfully a little bit miserable.

On the other hand, 40% of what I read shows teachers who love everything about their job. They see every classroom challenge as a chance to grow and every kid as a wonderful addition to their classroom. Let's be honest, who feels that way after teaching all day. These posts start to bring on the slight nausea. If you are a teacher who doesn't admit that you are happy when a certain student is absent then you certainly are a step ahead of me. If you listen intently at staff meetings and professional development without doodling in your notebook or playing on your phone then once again, I owe you a round of applause. I try to listen in meetings, but the truth is I'm fried by the end of the day. I'm interested in learning new things and expanding my toolkit but I can't successfully chase all 30 new initiatives the principal and district are pushing this year.

I'm writing this section for teachers like me that don't identify with either of these two extremes. A lot of us are right there in the middle of the road. We entered teaching to make a difference and some days we do, but other days teaching feels like a job that we wouldn't do if we didn't get paid. Just like other jobs, teaching always has its pros and cons. On the bad days, I remind myself that my students leave at 3p.m. and I don't have to take them home. On the good days, I realize that I'm making memories that these middle schoolers will have for a lifetime. In between the good and bad days,

I have lots of days that are just days, some kids learn, some kids avoid doing work, some papers get graded, other papers get recycled and then the day is done. Reading most teaching posts makes me feel sad that all teachers seem to have to fit in one of these categories. I pride myself on being balanced teacher. Every day I give teaching 100% of what I am capable of that day. Most days my lessons have videos, smooth transitions and a high level of student interest in activities. Some days I selfishly plan lessons that are easy for me. I don't always feel like cutting out stations, having choices and engaging multiple intelligences. Some days I have a headache and I feel the kids need to own their own learning and it's not my job to entertain them. Does that make me a bad teacher? I don't think so, I think these days make me human. Being human makes me a more balanced teacher and less likely to be a teacher who suffers from burnout.

Instead of showing off that we are superheroes all the time, I think all teachers need to realize and admit that they too are human and start giving themselves a break. You can have a few crossword puzzles and video days without being a shame to the profession. You can also acknowledge the challenges of public education without losing sleep over them. Rock on if you identify as a middle of the road teacher. You're doing the best you can given the less than perfect circumstances you are provided.

Reasons why middle school can be great

After reading this book, I hope you are feeling better about Middle School. For all of its challenges it can be a great place to work and learn. Teaching middle school often reminds me of my favorite quote from Alice and Wonderland, "But I don't want to go among mad people," Alice remarked. "Oh, you can't help that," said the Cat: "we're all mad here. I'm mad. You're mad." Truth be told successful middle school teachers aren't crazy, they just realize their limitations and the limitations of the students they teach. Put all these ideas in perspective and you can see the greatness of middle school.

Middle School is Great Because
1. It's never boring at work.
2. Students are old enough to know what's going on in the world and make connections, but young enough to enjoy games, simulations and group activities
3. You have other teachers who can help you become a better educator
4. You only have to master one subject to teach
5. They will learn everything you teach them again in high school so you don't have to feel pressured for them to master everything
6. Students leave after 45 minutes and the work day ends around 3p.m.
7. You get summers off, snow days, spring break, Thanksgiving break, Winter Break, President's Day, etc.
8. You get to watch students grow physically and academically during the school year.
9. You see students do great things in high school and later in life and feel proud
10. It matters! You can be a positive role model and help students through a difficult growth period. They

remember the way you made them feel and they take the academic skills you teach with them forever.

I have been teaching over 15 years. So, is it easy now? Every day I deal with 152 hormonal 7th graders, 134 cell phones, 152 of each paper to grade, 22 kids without a pencil, eight kids that need to make up work, and forms to fill out for four students who may need to go through educational screening. In case that is not clear, it's not easy. Teaching will always be challenging because of the large number of variables and decisions we make daily. Over the years I have developed different aspects of my teaching skill and if I look back, I will feel proud of my accomplishments. Teaching middle school is a great rewarding profession, but teaching will never be easy.

Best wishes as you pursue your teaching journey. It may not be easy, but it will be worth it. You have what it takes to be a great teacher, and your students are lucky to have you.

Acknowledgements

Thank you to my readers who have taken an interest in reading my book. This topic is so close to my heart and I'm glad to share it with you.

"I am the vine and you are the branches. If you remain in me and I in you, you will bear much fruit." John 15:5 Jesus-thank you for giving me this opportunity to be your branches.

Thank you to all my teacher friends like Shannon, Ruth, Amy, Cherie, Nora, Bev, Rob, Kate, Steven, Brian and others who have made me a better middle school teacher.

Thank you Marymac and Mandy for reading and editing.

Thank you, Buddy and Bear who have shown me the world, from a whole new perspective.

Thank you, Kevin, for being my better half and biggest supporter in every way.

Made in United States
North Haven, CT
22 December 2023

46405814R00098